Rosemarkie Connections

Freda Bassindale

Bassman Books

Published by Bassman Books, Burnside Cottage, Newhall, Balblair, Dingwall, IV7 8LT

First published in 2015

A catalogue record for this book is available from the British Library

ISBN 978-0-9567908-7-3

Printed by Big Sky, The Press Building, 305 The Park, Findhorn, Forres, IV36 3TE

Layout and Design: www.russellturner.org
Set in 11/13pt Palatino

By the same Author

Rosemarkie People and Places
ISBN 978-0-9567908-4-2

Contents

Dedicated to Elizabeth Sutherland, writer and historian, who set up the Black Isle Writers in 1986 and who still takes an active interest in the group. Over the years she has encouraged me and advised me, and her guidance has given me the confidence to publish this book

Introduction

No sooner had *Rosemarkie People and Places* hit the bookshelves than people were asking, "When's the next one coming out?" I needed to take some time out as the previous few months had been hectic and I was enjoying basking in the praise and good wishes that were coming my way.

As the months passed, I started to get restless. I put out a few feelers and I soon realised that there was a lot of history in Rosemarkie and its environs, and Rosemarkie Church seemed to be a good place to start.

I knew about the three generations of ministers, and I knew we had a famous veteran of the Afghan War buried in the churchyard, but not much else. Having a look round the church, I discovered several plaques commemorating a local family and in the churchyard I discovered a number of gravestones commemorating some interesting people. What I wasn't prepared for was the fantastic "journey" I would make from Rosemarkie to the slave plantations in Jamaica and to India and the infamous siege of Lucknow.

There was a lot more research needed for this book and I am indebted to the staff at the Highland Archives in Inverness for their help. Nothing was too much trouble for them and their expertise made my research enjoyable and fruitful. John Durham of the Highland Family History Society was also always willing to answer my questions.

A great deal of my research was carried out on-line. There are many records available such as Forces War Records, The National Archives, British Newspaper Archive, London Gazette, Oxford Biographical Dictionary, Scotland's People, Ancestry, Findmypast, Fibis and others.

Information on the slave industry of Jamaica was gleaned from the Jamaican Family Search Genealogy Research Library, a site compiled and maintained over a period of thirty years by an enthusiastic lady in Jamaica. This site is now administered by University College London and I am grateful to Dr Nicholas Draper of UCL for permission to use the information in this book. Dr David Alston's website, *Slaves and Highlanders* provided information on the British Guiana slave trade, and my thanks go to him for permission to use it.

Of course, many writers have chronicled the lives of several of the people featured, and the information contained in the following has been invaluable to me: *The Forgotten Victor: General Sir Richard O'Connor* by John Baynes; *The Last Man* by John Cunningham; *Diary of the Doctor's Lady* by Geoffrey Moore; *Hindu Koh* by Major-General D Macintyre VC; *Genealogical Tables of the Clan MacKenzie* by James D MacKenzie. I also refreshed my memory of local events by re-reading *Random Notes of Old Rosemarkie* by Alistair S Fraser, JP; *Fortrose and Rosemarkie Golf Club (125th Anniversary publication)* and *The Chanonry of Ross* by C G Macdowall.

My thanks also go to the staff of Inverness Library, Elgin Library and Elgin Museum for their help in tracing newspaper articles and making suggestions on other sources. The Moray Council Heritage Society's index to sources of information, *Libindex*, was also of help.

I was lucky enough to make contact with living relatives of some of the people in this book. John Fowler of Boulder, Connecticut, USA has been researching the Fowlers of Raddery and hopes to establish a connection between himself and the family. Ione and Emma Tayler, who still own MacKenzie Cottage in Fortrose, allowed me to view the cottage which contains some of the trophies of Donald Macintyre and many of his watercolours of the Himalayas. Alistair Macintyre, of Reykjavik, Iceland, also a descendant of Donald Macintyre, sent me a copy of his *Letterbain*

Narrative, a precis of research he has done for family consumption. Andrew MacKenzie of the Clan MacKenzie Society sent me excerpts from his book on the history of the MacKenzies, *May We Be Britons*. My thanks go to them all.

No book on Rosemarkie would be possible without the contributions of the local inhabitants and I am grateful to the following, including several not living in Rosemarkie but with a connection to the area, who have been patiently answering my questions, allowing me use of their photographs and being extremely helpful in many ways: Betty Marshall; Isobel Grigor; Jenny Paterson; Sheila Paterson; Helen Robinson; Ann Geddes; Mary Chalmers; Duncan Grigor; Mark and Edith Grigor; Alisdair Fraser (Flowerburn); Fran Tilbrook (Cromarty); Ruth MacGregor (nee Newall); Janice MacLeman (Avoch); Su Wompra (Groam House Museum); Stuart Edmond; Anne MacIver; Okain MacLennan; Mary Bisset; Joy Bisset; Sandy Jack (Dorset); Billy MacKay (Fortrose British Legion); the late George Taylor (Fortrose); Sheena Munro; John MacDonald (Australia); Ethel Urquhart; Graham and Genevieve MacIver; Glad MacIver; Grace MacKenzie (Fortrose); Donnie and Katy-Mary Sutherland (Fortrose); Catherine Patience (Avoch); Murdo MacPhail; Lorna Kemp (Avoch); Sylvia Brooks.

John MacKenzie, administrator of *Fortrose and Rosemarkie Past Images* has been particularly helpful in finding, at short notice, some of the photos I needed.

Finally, my thanks to Violet Jardine for her editing advice and to Ian Basham for his proof-reading skills. Last but not least, thanks to Russell Turner of *Bassman Books* for transforming a Word document and a bunch of photographs into the finished article that is *Rosemarkie Connections*.

If I've missed anyone, I'm sorry!

Note: In the 18th and 19th Centuries, some of the place names had a different spelling from that which is used today, for example Balmungy, Rosemarky. Where appropriate I have used the earlier spelling.

Freda Bassindale
November 2015

Rosemarkie Parish Church

Rosemarkie is full of history and the deeper I delve, the more I discover. From the earliest days the church played an important part in the life of the community. The church authorities regarded themselves as the people's moral and spiritual guardians; they looked after the poor and they also acted as bankers, lending money to local businessmen by way of the issue of bonds, the interest on which was paid annually or quarterly, or sometimes simply when the borrower had the means to do so. Mr Munro of Poyntzfield is recorded as having paid ten pounds ten shillings as two years' interest on his bond. This interest was sometimes paid in kind. In the Kirk Session minutes of 10th July 1780, Andrew Miller is recorded as "...*having paid money to the session in eight bolls of meal ... distributed in the Parish.*"

Prior to the state's official records, begun in 1855, the church faithfully recorded every birth, marriage and death in the Parish. Our social history would be sadly lacking if it were not for the diligence of the church ministers and clerks in the past.

A great deal of information on Rosemarkie Parish Church already exists, so enough to say that a church is believed to have stood on the present site since the 6th Century when Rosemarkie was an important part of the early Pictish/Celtic culture.

In the late 17th Century, Rosemarkie Church was lucky enough to benefit from the largesse of the House of Seaforth. In 1686 Isabella, Countess of Seaforth, presented two silver cups to Rosemarkie Church. They are believed to have been made by James Cockburn of Edinburgh, a well-known silversmith of the time, and bear the Edinburgh hallmark.

The bell in the present church tower was donated to the previous building by the Reverend John Wood. The bell is inscribed "*Cast for the Church of Rosemarky 1753. This bell was presented by Mr John Wood, Minister of Town and Parishes."* The photo of the bell was given by Stuart Edmond.

The foundation stone of the present building was laid on 18th June 1819 and the completed building was opened on 12th August 1821. The first marriage to take place there was on 28th December 1821 between William Bain, labourer in Balmungy, and Janet Anderson. After the official entry in the Marriage Register, the Session Clerk, John MacRae, helpfully added the following note: *"N.B. This was the first couple whose marriage was solemnized in the new church of this Parish of Rosemarkie, opened for public worship on the twelfth day of August last, namely, one thousand eight hundred and twenty one years."*

When Rosemarkie Church was built, it didn't have a clock and at a meeting of the Town Council on 24th May 1887 it was agreed that a clock would be purchased. Baillies John Hossack and George Sutherland, Treasurer Geddie and the Town Clerk formed a sub-committee, tasked with making enquiries and getting estimates for supplying a clock to be placed in the tower of the church. The Town Clerk wrote to the minister, Mr McDowall, telling him what was proposed and asking if he had any objections to the proposal.

Two weeks later, Mr McDowall replied to the council that *"...I believe that neither the Kirk Session nor the Heritors of the Parish of Rosemarkie can have any objection to the proposal."* It doesn't sound as if he actually asked them!

As the Town Clerk was going to London, it was suggested that he call at a leading clockmaker to ascertain if a suitable clock could be found. It would appear that the size of clock required was the last thing on the minds of the committee, because the clerk came back saying that Sir John Bennett, Clockmaker, wanted to know the size of the clock tower. The enquiries couldn't have gone that well, because the clerk said that from his conversations with the clockmaker, a more satisfactory and more economical outcome would be to get estimates from local clockmakers. The sub-

The Rosemarkie Church bell.

committee was then tasked with getting the dimensions of the clock tower and obtaining estimates from clockmakers in Inverness, but also *"...from one or two leading firms in the south."* Someone wasn't convinced that local firms could do the job.

On 15th August 1887 the following estimates were put before the Town Council:
● Sir John Bennett, London for a turret clock – £65.0.0
● Sir John Bennett, for a clock to strike on a bell already fixed in the tower – £100.0.0
● Ferguson and McBean, Inverness for a turret clock – £51.15.0
● Ferguson and McBean for a smaller turret clock – £46.10.0

After consideration, it was decided that the clerk would write to Messrs Ferguson and McBean to ask if the clock would strike and, if not, to state the extra cost for a striking clock. The clerk was also authorised to *"...write to Mr Scott of Newton, Cromarty for the sum in his hands belonging to the Minor Heritors Fund as the Town Council have arranged to get a clock for Rosemarkie."* In due course the sum of one hundred pounds, four shillings and fivepence was received from Mr Scott. The cost of the clock was seventy pounds, twelve shillings, with the remainder of the money to be spent on the drains in Fortrose.

There were conditions attached to Messrs Ferguson and McBean getting the contract. The clock had to be fixed to the bell already in place in the tower, and they had to guarantee the clock for five years. Messrs Ferguson and McBean said they couldn't agree to a five year guarantee, but after discussion they did agree, provided the person appointed to look after the clock was given instructions by themselves.

By 13th February 1888, the clock was in place and the account was received. The Town Council only agreed to pay on the proviso that a representative from Messrs Ferguson and McBean met with the clock sub-committee so that they could point out *"...a few defects ...which in their opinion could be improved."* Councillor John Gordon, Rosemarkie, offered to pay twenty-one pounds towards the cost of the clock, and this was gratefully received.

But this was not the end of the tale of the clock. Baillie Sutherland submitted some accounts for wood and other articles used in connection with setting the new clock in place. By this time, the Council had apparently spent the money they received from the fund and from Councillor John Gordon, because the clerk reported that *"...there was no money in the hands of the Burgh Authorities belonging to the clock fund and as it was understood the contractor for the clock was to have made everything complete, these accounts were ordered to lie on the table meantime."*

A month later, Baillie Sutherland pressed for payment, and explained that the accounts were for wood and other articles ordered by the committee for finishing the platform under the clock, which was needed to enable the clock-keeper to wind the clock.

The original mechanism of Rosemarkie Church's clock.

The accounts were:
- Hugh Home, Merchant, Rosemarkie – £0.18.2
- James Walker & Co Timber Merchants, Inverness – £1.2.6

The Council authorised payment and, thankfully, that was the last of the saga of the clock.

In 1972, Fortrose Town Council had problems finding someone to sound the curfew in Fortrose Cathedral and decided to automate the system. At the same time it was decided to update the Rosemarkie clock and replace the heavy workings with a more modern electronic mechanism. An estimate of five hundred and sixty pounds was received from Smiths of Derby. The existing dial gearing and striking hammer were cleaned and overhauled and an electricity supply fitted. The old machinery was removed and this magnificent piece of redundant iron and brass is now on display in the gallery at the rear of Rosemarkie Church. The bell is still in the turret but is now redundant as the clock no longer strikes.

The Wood Family

On 2nd August 1815, a new Record Book for the Parish of Rosemarkie was begun by the Reverend Alexander Wood and Thomas Bain, Session Clerk. Records covering the period 1780 to 1815 were missing, and an entry in the new book recorded: *"The blank that occurs in the books between 1780 and 1815 is caused by the fact that the house of the Grammar Schoolmaster in Fortrose was burned, he being at the time Session Clerk of the Parish – it was understood that the books and papers in his possession were there and then destroyed by the fire."*

On the opening page, the records of the previous ministers of the parish were brought up to date, and it recorded that three successive generations of the Wood family ministered in Rosemarkie Church over a period of a hundred and thirty-four years.

The first of these, the Reverend John Wood, was born 8th March 1704 in the parish of Fordyce, in Banff, and he served as minister of Rosemarkie from 5th August 1734, until his death on 10th November 1775 aged seventy-one.

In 1739 John married Ann Ogilvie. The Session Clerk recorded in the Church Register, the marriage of John and Ann: *"The Reverend John Wood, Minister of this parish, and Ann Ogilvie, daughter of Collector Ogilvie of the Shire of Banff, were contracted in order to marriage, and, after having been regularly proclaimed, their marriage was solemnized on the fifth day of April, in the year one thousand seven hundred and thirty-nine."*

On the same page of the register, and immediately below the marriage entry, is a record of the death of Ann six years later: *"The said Ann Ogilvie departed this life at the Manse of Rosemarkie, on the twenty-seventh day of April, one thousand seven hundred and forty-five years, leaving no surviving issue: Her Remains were interred in the family burying ground at Rosemarkie."*

A commemorative wall plaque, in stone and wood, hangs in the vestry in Rosemarkie Church in memory of Ann Ogilvie, who, according to the Latin inscription, died whilst giving birth to her daughter Helena. As the previous death record shows, Ann left no surviving issue, so presumably Helena died at birth.

Two years later, on 17th June 1747, John married for a second time. This marriage is the third entry recorded on the same page of the Register, and immediately below the death of Ann Ogilvie. John's new wife, Sophia Irvine, was the daughter of the Reverend Alexander Irvine of Elgin.

Born on 7th April 1731 in Auldearn, where her father was the minister, Sophia celebrated her seventeenth birthday just ten weeks before her marriage to John, who was aged forty-three. Poor Sophia! Was this an arranged marriage? John Wood was of similar age to Sophia's father, the Reverend Alexander Irvine, and they were from the same village, so would have been acquainted.

The records go on to show that between October 1748 and July 1772, Sophia gave birth to nine sons and two daughters! She lived a long life, however, and died in May 1803 aged seventy-three. A marble wall plaque commemorating the life of the Rev John Wood and Sophia, was erected the following year in the vestry by their son Joseph, resident in Jamaica. It is placed next to the plaque in memory of Ann Ogilvie.

John Wood became ill at the beginning of February 1772, and according to the Session Minutes, his son the Reverend Alexander Wood had already taken over the duties of Moderator. There had been a problem with the church collections. The minutes of the Kirk Session dated 6th July 1772 recorded: *"The Moderator reported … at present there could be no exact account of the collections from 2nd July 1771 to the 1st February 1772 owing to his father's indisposition which has great-*

The Reverend Alexander Wood, son of Alexander Wood.

ly hurt his memory." The Reverend Alexander Wood also informed the session that he *"would endeavour (if possible) to obtain a particular account of the above collections and at any rate he should take care that the Session suffers no loss."*

The congregation was not averse to a bit of chicanery on occasion. Dotted throughout the reports by the Moderator, when recording the amount in the collection, he records that, for example, the sum of three pounds, eight and ninepence was collected in good coin and eighteen shillings and three-pence in bad coin *"thrown in among the rest."*

The Reverend John Wood passed away on 10th November 1775 aged seventy-one and, on his death, his son Alexander Wood was appointed to the post. Alexander married Janet Houston, eldest daughter of the late Alexander Houston, Provost of Fortrose, on 4th December 1773. The records have no entries for the birth of any children to Alexander and Janet, but they had at least three: Alexander, Sophia and Janet.

Alexander and Janet's elder daughter, Sophia, married James Fowler of Jamaica in Rosemarkie Parish Church on 29th December 1792. The Fowler family was resident in Raddery and James Fowler and his two brothers feature later in this book.

On the death of Alexander Wood on 22nd August 1809, his son, also called Alexander, did not automatically succeed to the post. The following announcement appeared in the *Inverness Journal* dated 29th September 1809: *"The King has been pleased to present the Reverend Alexander Wood to the Church and Parish of Rosemarkie, in the Presbytery of Chanonry and County of Ross, vacant by the death of Mr Alexander Wood, late minister there."* However, there then began five-and-a-half years of protracted litigation respecting the patronage.

The cause of the litigation was probably a dispute over the choice of minister. On 1st May 1712 the Lay Patronage Act was introduced by Parliament. This put the power for the appointment of ministers into the hands of a few large prop-erty holders, and this law became the source of many divi-sions in the Church for more than a century, leading to the Great Disruption of 1843. It wasn't until 1874, thirty-one years after the Disruption, that the Lay Patronage Act was repealed and the church regained greater control of its affairs.

During the five-and-a-half years mentioned above, Alexander Wood, according to the Session Minutes, carried out the duties of the parish minister in an unofficial capacity until he was formally appointed to the post. He was eventually ordained in the post in August 1815 and in the Record Book dated 2nd August 1815, Session Clerk Thomas Bain recorded: *"During this long and anxious period of the vacancy, Mr Wood, the present incumbent, continued to discharge all the duties that befell to him to perform in the parish, as a preacher of the Gospel, which he did."*

Alexander Wood went on to serve the parish for sixty-four years until his death in 1874 aged eighty-eight. He married Agnes Walker, daughter of Adam Walker of Muirhouselaw in Roxburghshire on 18th December 1821. Agnes gave birth to three children: Alexander, born 31st December 1822; Catherine Gaird, born 26th October 1824; and Jannetta Fowler, born 6th June 1826. Agnes died on 27th March 1861 aged sixty-nine years.

In 1932, Miss Katie Rose of Chester, a descendant of the Wood family, made a gift of two portraits in oils of the Reverend Alexander Wood and his wife, Agnes. In the entry in the Session Minutes recording receipt of this gift, the clerk recorded: *"The portraits are considered excellent likenesses by parishioners still alive in the parish who knew the Reverend Alexander Wood and his wife."* The portraits have been cleaned and restored and now hang in Rosemarkie Church.

The Reverend James McDowall had been ordained assistant and successor on 9th May 1861, and on the death of Alexander Wood on 8th January 1874 he succeeded to the post, thereby ending the succession of the Wood family.

Agnes Walker, wife of the second Alexander Wood.

Rosemarkie's War Dead

Rosemarkie, like so many other small communities in the Highlands, suffered a heavy toll in young lives during the two World Wars. In the village today, there are countless family group photographs, each of which includes at least one young man in uniform, standing beside his parents and siblings, preparing to go to war. Many families took advantage of the travelling photographers to have family photographs taken, no doubt in the belief that they might not see their loved ones again, and wanted to remember them.

Inside the main door of Rosemarkie Church is a metal plaque commemorating those members of the congregation who made the ultimate sacrifice.

Brothers **Alexander and James Sutherland** fell in the Great War. Alexander and James were both born in Glasgow to John Sutherland, a stonecutter, and his wife Christina MacKenzie. The family moved, first to Inverness where they can be found in the 1901 Census, living at 13 Greig Street. They moved shortly after this date to Holmes Cottage, High Street, Rosemarkie, where John Sutherland died on 27th June 1902.

Alexander joined 14th (County of London) Battalion, London Scottish and was killed in action in France on 1st July 1916 aged twenty-four. He is buried in the Thiepval Memorial Cemetery, France.

The action in which Alexander lost his life was centred on the village of Thiepval. Thirteen divisions of Commonwealth forces were involved and despite a bombardment lasting seven days the German defences were barely touched. The initial attack was a colossal failure and losses were catastrophic. Huge resources of manpower and equipment were subsequently deployed by the Allies, but strong resistance from the enemy meant that, at the end of September, Thiepval was finally captured by the Germans.

The plaque which honours Rosemarkie's war dead.

James joined the Cameron Highlanders and was serving with the 5th Battalion in France when he was killed in action on 23rd March 1918 aged nineteen. According to the Graves Registration Form, he was buried in Tincourt New British Cemetery, Picardy, France.

Tincourt was one of several villages which were occupied by British troops in March 1917 during the German retreat to the Hindenberg Line. From May 1917 until March 1918, the village became a Casualty Clearing Station. On 23rd March 1918 the villages were evacuated and were not recovered until 6th September, in a ruined condition. It would appear that James lost his life during this evacuation.

The following notice appeared in the *Aberdeen Journal* dated 10th September 1927: "*Mrs Sutherland, Home's Close, Rosemarkie has been notified by the War Office that the remains of her younger son, Private James Sutherland of the Cameron*

No. 5 Area, I.W.G.C.
Serial No. 90.
20/1/25.

Army Form W. 3372.

GRAVES REGISTRATION REPORT FORM.

COMPREHENSIVE REPORT.
REPORT No. 4. SCHEDULE No. 1286.

COMMUNE:- TINCOURT BOUCLY.

PLACE OF BURIAL   TINCOURT NEW BRITISH CEMETERY.

Map Reference   62c. J.23. b.4.7.

The following are buried here:—

Plot 7, Row "..." G 7/1996

Regiment	No.	Name	Rank and Initials	Date of Death	Cross Erected or G.R. U'd	Plot, Row and Grave / Grave No.
5/D.G.		UNKNOWN BRITISH SOLDIER.		-	E.	12.
Manchesters.Regt		UNKNOWN BRITISH SOLDIER.		-	E.	13.
23/Manchesters.	22689	MITCHELL.	Pte- H.	25/7/16.	E.	14.
Kings.		UNKNOWN BRITISH SOLDIER.		-	E.	15.
5/R.Berks. attd m/Manc.R.	21000 DANCE Pte W.	UNKNOWN BRITISH SOLDIER.		30-7-16	E.	16.
		UNKNOWN BRITISH SOLDIER.		-	E.	17.
Manchesters.Regt		UNKNOWN BRITISH SOLDIER.		-	E.	18.
R.H.A. Pte.	15657	KENNEDY.	Pte J	1-7-16		19.
Row "..."						
145/H.B. R.G.A.	109511	BROWN	Gnr.F.A.H.	18/9/18	E.	8.
31b/Bde.R.F.A.	695873	DYSON	Gnr. N.R.	20/9/18	E.	9.
-do.-	262921	CLARK	Gnr. N.	20/9/18	E.	10.
-do.-	50364	SOUTHAN	Sgt. W.	20/9/18	E.	11.
12/R.Scots.	S/31209 42022	SUTHERLAND	Pte. J.	23-3-18		12.
R.A.M.C.		RYLEY	Major. C.	4/5/17	E.	13.
S.African Sig.Co.9701		FOGARTY	Spr. T.	10/4/17	E.	14.
S Co.21/Middx.Regt.15758		FLOWER	L/Cpl.T.C.	10/4/17	E.	15.

Graves registration for for Private James Sutherland.

Highlanders, killed in Action in France on March 23rd 1918, have been found and identified by his disc."

Lance Corporal O'Kain MacLennan S/40417 was born at Easter Suddie, in the parish of Knockbain on 2nd November 1877 to Murdoch MacLennan and his wife Margaret Cameron.

O'Kain has an interesting military history. He enlisted in the Gordon Highlanders on 8th February 1900 and his military record places him in a "depot" appointment. On 6th May 1901, he embarked for South Africa for action in the Second Boer War. This engagement lasted until 22nd October 1902, when O'Kain was awarded the South Africa Medal and Clasp for service in Cape Colony, Orange Free State and Transvaal.

On 17th July 1902, whilst serving in South Africa, O'Kain was promoted to Corporal and on 2nd September 1902, he transferred to the 1st Battalion Gordon Highlanders. In October, that same year, a week after his return from South Africa, O'Kain reverted to the rank of Private *"at his own request"*. His record doesn't give the reason for this.

On 27th March 1905, O'Kain extended his period of service to twelve years and on the same day he was promoted Lance Corporal *"in the pipes"*. He became a piper in the Gordon Highlanders Pipe Band.

When he married his wife Jessie Ross in Avoch on 6th June 1905, O'Kain was stationed in Cork, Ireland. O'Kain's father was working as a gamekeeper on the Rosehaugh Estate, and Jessie may also have been working at

Rosehaugh as she gave her address as Mid Lodge, Rosehaugh, Avoch, which is where the marriage took place.

On 25th February 1907, O'Kain was on the move again when he transferred to the 3rd Battalion Seaforth Highlanders in the rank of Private. On the same date he was appointed "*Drummer*" so presumably he was now in the Seaforth Highlanders pipe band.

O'Kain went on to have three children between 1905 and 1909: Helen Sutherland, born on 15th August 1905 at Avoch; Margaret Ann Cameron, born on 1st March 1908 at Dingwall, and Elizabeth Ann Ross, born on 31st December 1909 at Rosehaugh. It is interesting to note that the Army recorded the dates of birth of all the children, where they were born and where and when they were christened and by whom.

On 7th February 1912, O'Kain completed his full twelve years' service and was discharged under paragraph 390 (xxi) of the King's Regulations.

When the First World War started in 1914, O'Kain joined the 7th Battalion Seaforth Highlanders in the rank of Lance Corporal. Presumably because of his previous twelve years' service in the Gordons and the Seaforths, and his experience of action in the Second Boer War, he was able to assume immediately the responsibilities of this non-commissioned rank.

Because of the loss of many of the records of the First World War, in the London Blitz, we have no details of O'Kain's service, except that he enlisted at Fort George. He died, aged thirty-eight, on 11th April 1917, in the first Battle of Arras, and was buried nearby in the Aubigny Communal Cemetery Extension. Aubigny-en-Artois is a village about fifteen kilometres north-west of Arras and from March 1916 until the Armistice, Aubigny was held by Commonwealth troops. Burials were carried out there until September 1918

O'Kain was awarded the British War Medal and the Victory Medal, but these were not automatically sent to the

Cambrai War Memorial, Louverval. It holds the remains of 7,057 casualties.

family of those who had been killed. His family, however, would have been sent a Death Penny and accompanying certificate.

Private James Ross, 7129, 2nd Battalion Seaforth Highlanders is also commemorated on the plaque in Rosemarkie Church. James died on 14th September 1914 and was buried in the Crouy-Vauxrot French National Cemetery, at Crouyaisne, France. There are fifty First World War casualties commemorated at this site, nearly half of whom are unidentified. All fell in September and October 1914.

Private Peter Smith, 1479, Highland Mounted Brigade, Field Ambulance, Royal Army Medical Corps was the son of Jemima Smith of High Street, Rosemarkie, and the late Finlay Smith. He was born in Strathpeffer and died on 27th January 1917 aged twenty-two. He was buried at the Cairo

Sgt Alexander Jack in the uniform of the Seaforth Highlanders.

War Memorial Cemetery, which is situated about five kilometres south east of the centre of Cairo.

At the outbreak of the First World War, Cairo was headquarters to the UK garrison in Egypt and, with Alexandria, became the main hospital centre for Gallipoli in 1915, dealing later with the sick and wounded from operations in Egypt and Palestine. There are two thousand and fifty-six Commonwealth casualties of the war buried or commemorated in the cemetery.

Private Duncan Cameron Ross, 1777, 4th Battalion Seaforth Highlanders was the son of Thomas and Flora Ross of 2 High Street, Rosemarkie. He was killed on 9th May 1915, aged twenty. He is commemorated in Le Touret Memorial at Pas de Calais, France.

Sergeant Alexander Jack, 200066, 4th Battalion Seaforth Highlanders, a cousin of Jenny Paterson, Rosemarkie, was born at Holmes Close, Rosemarkie, on 16th August 1894, to Donald Jack, Master Blacksmith, and his wife Martha Moir.

Alick, as he was known, was employed as a blacksmith in Evanton and joined the 4th Battalion Seaforths in 1912. He went out to France in November 1914 and saw some severe fighting in which he was wounded on three occasions in different engagements.

Alick was killed on 19th September 1918 aged twenty-three and is commemorated on the Tyne Cot Memorial at Zonnebeke, Belgium, one of four memorials to the missing in Flanders. Tyne Cot bears the names of almost thirty-five thousand officers and men whose graves are not known.

The following letter was written by Alick's Company Commander to his mother, Martha: "*Dear Mrs Jack, In the sad bereavement which overshadows your home at this time I extend to you my deepest sympathy. You have lost a son and we, a soldier whose bravery and keenness all admired and even envied. Sergeant Jack was one of the most highly respected of N.C.O.s in this battalion, and one of the few remaining who linked the tradition of pride of the original members with those of today. On the morning of the attack we went forward together, and none know better than I of the work that he did as once again we struck at those who would suppress our most sacred principles. It was while consolidating the ground won that your son was hit. His death was sudden and painless, and occurred just as our task was done. Officers, N.C.O.s and men join me in the expression of our deepest sympathy to you and your sorrowing family."*

Alick was awarded the British War Medal and the Victory Medal. His family received the Death Penny awarded to the next of kin of all those who fell in the Great War.

Corporal John Hossack, 200156, of the 4th Battalion Seaforth Highlanders was born on 25th May 1895 at Rosemarkie to Robert Hossack, general labourer, and his wife Elizabeth. John fell on 20th November 1917, on the first day of the Battle of Cambrai. He was twenty-two.

The fighting began early in the morning. In this battle, a new method of assault was introduced where there was no preliminary artillery bombardment. Instead, tanks were used to break through the German wire while the infantry followed under cover of smoke barrages. Initial advances were successful and on 22nd November a halt was called for rest and reorganisation. Unfortunately, this also allowed the Germans to reinforce their lines. Fighting continued for six days in the area called Bourbon Wood, but by 29th November it was clear that the Germans were ready for a major counter attack, and after a further five days of fierce fighting, most of the ground gained by the British in the early days of the attack, was lost.

John is commemorated in the Cambrai Memorial, Louverval, France, a memorial which commemorates over seven thousand servicemen of the UK and South Africa who died in the battle of Cambrai and whose graves are not known.

Private Alexander More, 267331, 1st/6th Battalion Seaforth Highlanders died 21st November 1917 and is buried at Rocquigny-Equancourt Road British Cemetery,

The Death Penny received by the family of Private Roderick Bisset.

Manancourt, Somme, France.

Lance Corporal Alexander J Munro, 225742, 10th Battalion Cameron Highlanders, was the nephew of Mr A D Munro of Balmungie. He died on 13th May 1918, aged twenty-three, and is buried in Mikra British Cemetery, Kalamaria, Greece. The cemetery now contains one thousand, eight hundred and ten Commonwealth burials from the First World War.

Private Daniel B Fraser, 1964, Seaforth Highlanders, was born in Cromarty but lived in Rosemarkie. He died on 9th May 1915 and is buried in Le Touret Memorial, Pas de Calais, France. This memorial commemorates thirteen thousand, four hundred and two casualties who were killed in the Western Front between the beginning of October 1914 and the eve of the Battle of Loos, in late September 1915.

Another Rosemarkie soldier who is not mentioned on the church plaque is **Private Roderick Bisset, S/40422, of the 7th Battalion Seaforth Highlanders** who was born in Wester Raddery, near Rosemarkie and whose sisters Isa and Lizzie lived in the High Street.

Roddy fell on 9th April 1917 on the first day of the first battle of Arras, a British offensive which involved British, Canadian, New Zealand, Newfoundland and Australian troops. The objective was to draw German troops away from an area chosen for a massive French attack under the command of General Robert Nivelle. The planned assault began a day late and was carried out in sleet and snow until darkness fell, preventing further advance.

Roddy was aged aged twenty-six when he was killed. He is buried in Point-du-Jour Military Cemetery, Athies, Pas de Calais, France. Athies is a village near to Arras in the Scarpe Valley and was captured by the 9th Scottish Division on 9th April. It remained in Allied hands for the remainder of the war.

Point-du-Jour Military Cemetery, Athies, Pas de Calais, France. This cemetery holds 396 identified war dead.

The Fowlers of Raddery

There are several plaques in Rosemarkie Church commemorating the Fowlers of Raddery and they turn out to be an interesting family. Brothers John, Andrew and James Fowler owned several estates in Jamaica during the 18th and 19th centuries. The eldest brother, John Fowler of Friendship Estate, Parish of Trelawney, died in Jamaica in June 1792 aged thirty-seven.

Researching the Fowlers led to an interesting journey into life in the West Indies more than two hundred years ago. John Fowler was born circa 1755, but the records regarding his antecedents are scanty and there is no certainty as to where he was born or who his parents were. Neither is it known when he went to Jamaica, nor how he obtained his properties there.

On 5th May 1494 Christopher Columbus landed in Jamaica, on the spot he named Discovery Bay, and claimed the land in the name of the King and Queen of Spain. In 1509, fifteen years after that first visit to the island, Spanish colonists settled in the St Anne's Bay area, but their arrival was a disaster for the indigenous people, who were either killed or used as slaves.

In 1655, after a successful attack by the British, the Spaniards surrendered and fled to Cuba. British settlers then began to arrive on the island. These newcomers grew crops such as tobacco, indigo and cocoa, followed by sugar cane, which eventually became the main crop of the island. White settlers were encouraged to travel to Jamaica by the British Government, which introduced several Acts of Parliament granting them parcels of land on the island. This might have been when the first of the Fowler family received his land. An entry in the Return of Jamaican Land Grants 1735 to 1754 shows that, in 1748, three hundred acres of land in Norman's Valley, in the parish of St James, were granted to a William

The plaque commemorating the Fowlers of Raddery.

Fowler. In 1751 a James Fowler was granted three hundred acres adjacent to that owned by William Fowler. Unfortunately, neither of these Fowlers can be connected to our family in Raddery.

The Almanac and Register for the Island of Jamaica was published annually. In the 1784 edition, the list of Jamaica General and Staff Officers shows John Fowler as a Second Lieutenant in the Trelawney Midland Troup. In 1787 and 1790 he is listed as Captain John Fowler of the Trelawney Leeward Troup. As his name is at the top of the list, he is presumably the man in charge.

The records of the Jamaican Family Search Genealogy research library show that John Fowler, in his short life, had become a very successful and wealthy man. An inventory, part of the winding up of his affairs, states: *"From the inventory of John Fowler, dated 14th January 1793. Schedule A, being a list of Slaves, part of the estate of John Fowler, Esquire, deceased, of Friendship Estate and Thatch Hill Penn in the Parish of Trelawney."* The list names a total of a hundred and twenty-seven slaves, sixty-six of whom are male and sixty-one female. Many on the list are children.

Schedule B gives a list of the livestock on the two estates and this list includes *"…forty-six steers, five cows, twenty-six mules, eight horses, two colts and one Dunn mare and her two followers."*

John Fowler, of Boulder, Connecticut, is researching the Fowlers, and has copies of the original inventory documents. He comments regarding the inventory: *"This version also lists … an English Horse called Charger, which seems to be valued at £140. That's more than the value of most of John Fowler's slaves. Presumably it was his personal horse, and as a rich planter and captain in the Horse Militia he would have had the best, but it's a sad commentary that a horse was worth more than most of the slaves."*

Schedule C is *"…a list of Bonds, Notes and other Obligations which are part of the personal estate of John Fowler Esq., late of the parish of Trelawney, deceased."* This extensive list covers five pages and the total amounts to £74,374.19.6½ sterling, which was a significant sum in 1793.

John also became an agent for James Rogers and Company, and three shipments of slaves were delivered to him at Trelawney Port. The Jamaican Family Research Library shows that John took his job as agent seriously, as his letters to James Rogers show. In a letter dated 8th September 1790, John acknowledged the receipt of a hundred and forty-one slaves from Captain Goodrich of the *Sarah*. They are not "Eboes" (from Nigeria) which are the preferred slaves. He ends his letter, *"I shall be happy if Captain Goodrich is sent for a cargo of real Eboes, to consist of young people."* The next shipment by the *Sarah* consisted of Eboes, as per John's instructions. A third shipment arrived on the *Daniel*, a 126-ton brig registered in Bristol, during 1792, after the death of John.

There is no trace of a marriage for John Fowler, but an entry in the Parish Registers and Civil Registration of Jamaica, shows that on 30th December 1789, Sarah Williams Fowler was born to Sarah Williams, a *"free person of colour."* The father is shown as *"John Fowler, white."* Young Sarah's uncle, James Fowler of Raddery, may have taken on her care after John's death in 1792 and brought her to Raddery. Her marriage to George Budge, Quartermaster of the Ross-shire Militia is recorded in the Old Parish Records of Leith South on 29th August 1811. Poor Sarah did not have much luck in life, however, as a further entry in the same records states: *"Sarah Williams Fowler, relict of the deceased Mr George Budge, late Quartermaster of the Ross shire Militia, a posthumous daughter named Georgina, born 4th August and baptised 26th August 1813 before the congregation."* George Budge's death was recorded at Dalkeith on 20th August 1813, but presumably he died prior to the birth of his daughter on 4th August.

Sarah's death at Dulcie Bridge, Grantown on Spey, on 17th June 1816, aged twenty-six, is included in the Register of Deaths in the Parish of Rosemarkie where the late George Budge has mysteriously risen to the rank of Lieutenant! No further trace of Georgina has been found.

The records in the Highland Archives have revealed a codicil to the will of John Fowler. This original document, written on thick parchment in language redolent of the period, took a bit of deciphering. However, it states: *"I give unto the poor people dwelling in the Town of Fortrose, the sum of £100 to be paid into the hands of the Baillies of the said town to be by them distributed and to the new foundation or Charity for Instructing Youth, the sum of one hundred guineas at the same place to be paid one year after my decease. Signed J Fowler, 23 July 1791."*

There are three witnesses to the signing of the codicil and six executors, including John's two brothers. They certainly showed no due diligence in their execution of the will, however, because in September 1795 the money had not yet been paid to the Town Council. In the Minute of the Town Council meeting of 9th September that year, the clerk is requested to write to Messrs MacAndrew, Wright and Murray regarding *"…the bequest of the late John Fowler to the poor of Fortrose and ascertain from them what they would advise the Magistrates to do in order to recover payment of the sum or whether they think the amount should be struck off as irrecoverable."* It appears that the bequest to the new Fortrose Academy also failed to materialise.

Information on the second Fowler brother, Andrew, is very scarce. Notification of his death in *The Columbian Magazine* of June 1796 states that he died in 1796 at Armagh, in the Parish of Trelawney. Information from John Fowler of Boulder, Connecticut, is that Andrew Fowler died of wounds sustained in the only classical battle of the second Maroon War. Andrew was, at that time, a lieutenant in the Trelawney Light Horse, a militia unit which was badly mauled in an attack on the Maroon homeland in December 1795. The commanding officer of Andrew's detachment was killed and Andrew had to lead the remainder of the troop to safety.

After the death of his two brothers in Jamaica, James Fowler returned to his estate in Raddery and became an absentee landlord. James had married seventeen-year-old Sophia Wood, daughter of the Reverend Alexander Wood, on 29th December 1792 in Rosemarkie Parish Church. James was already resident in Jamaica and it would appear that Sophia joined him there, at least for a few years. Her two eldest children were born in Jamaica: John was born at Martha Brae, Trelawney on 26th March 1795, and Jannetta Andrina was born at Armagh House, Trelawney on 14th November 1796. Sophia's third child was born at the manse in Rosemarkie on 29th November 1798. A further ten children were born in Fortrose.

During the 17th and 18th centuries, Scotland was heavily involved in emigration to America and the West Indies and they were the places to go to make fortunes. Money was sent home to buy estates in Scotland and many of these estate owners became the benefactors of public buildings. Many schools, hospitals and churches are among the public buildings which were built during this time with money gained in the slave trade.

The Abolition of the Slave Trade Act came into effect on 25th March 1807. Although the Act made it illegal to engage in the slave trade throughout the British colonies, trafficking between the Caribbean islands continued and no attempt was made to free the existing slaves. It took almost twenty-six years for abolition to be fully effective. A negotiated settlement established apprenticeships for the freed men and women and compensation, amounting to £20m of taxpayers money (40% of the total Government budget for 1834) was paid to the slave-owners. No compensation was paid to slaves.

According to the Annual Returns of Proprietors, Properties, Slaves and Stock published in the *Jamaican*

Almanac of 1817, James Fowler owned three estates: Grange, Lottery and Friendship, and a total of four hundred and twenty-six slaves. By 1833 the number of slaves had risen to five hundred and seventy-seven.

In November 1835, James Fowler submitted five claims for compensation:
- Claim no. 39 for Friendship Estate where he owned 153 slaves, yielded £3,053.27.7.
- Claim no. 179 for Lottery Estate, where he owned 205 slaves, yielded £3,814.15.11
- Claim no. 181 for Grange Estate where he owned 141 slaves, yielded £2,868.10.9
- Claim no. 89 for St James where he owned four slaves, yielded £109.11.10
- Claim no. 90, also for St James where he owned six slaves, yielded £103.19.0.

In the *Almanac* for year 1838, the Annual Returns now list Proprietors, Properties and Apprentices. The compensation money was supposed to pay for apprenticeships for the many slaves on the plantations, but apparently, not much changed and the apprentices were tied to the plantations for many years to come, usually without pay.

In 1840, the Annual Returns no longer showed the number of apprentices on the estates, but they recorded the acreage. James Fowler's three estates amounted to 2,322 acres in total.

At home in Raddery, James took an active part in the local community, becoming a member of Fortrose Town Council in the early 1820s. He held the position of Provost for the year 1827 to 1828.

James Fowler died on 4th August 1842, aged seventy-nine, and was buried in Fortrose Cathedral. In his will, the executor, his son Henry MacKenzie Fowler, valued his personal belongings at £1,749.17.2 which included furniture and farm stock. Raddery Estate was valued at £1,500. There is no mention of any other property. A search for records of the sale of

Grange House, Trelawney – the home of James Fowler.

Lottery, Grange and Friendship met with no success. Neither was there any trace of the many thousands of pounds of compensation money.

James outlived all but four of his family. When his successor, his youngest son Henry MacKenzie Fowler, died in 1884, he was collecting rent from two cottages and eleven farms on the Black Isle: D. Young, **Muirden**; R Grigor, **Carse**; John Clark, **Craiglands**; John Clark, **Burnside;** A & W Watson, **Upper Raddery;** John Grigor, **Ryeflat;** A Grigor, **Craiglands** (may be Wester Craiglands); James Anderson, **Olddam;** John A Fowler, **Mains of Raddery;** H Clark, **Broomhill;** Colin Munro, **Weston.** Henry also owned shares in the Prairie Cattle Company.

The Prairie Cattle Company, according to the Texas State Historical Association, was established in 1880 by the Scottish American Mortgage Company, based in Edinburgh. By 1882 the company owned close to a hundred thousand

Interior of Rosemarkie Church showing the communion table.

cattle and range rights to an unbroken, 300-mile strip of land from the Canadian River to the Arkansas River.

The company prospered for a time but, in a fierce blizzard in January 1886, many of the cattle froze to death. The price of beef dropped and the company began selling off small parcels of land. By 1916 the Prairie Cattle Company, at one time the world's largest British Investment Company, had been liquidated.

When Henry MacKenzie Fowler died, Raddery was inherited by his son, James Evan Fowler. It would appear that James was an absentee landlord, as an item in the *Inverness Courier* dated 1st May 1891 reports that a farewell dinner was held in the Royal Hotel Fortrose, where "...*the tenants of Raddery Estate entertained their laird, James Evan Fowler who was returning to Travancore, Kerala, India after spending the last few months at Raddery.*" James had been resident in Travancore for fifteen years.

Some tragedy appears to have befallen James, perhaps when he was in India. An oak communion table in Rosemarkie Church was gifted to the church by his mother, Mrs Louisa Fowler. It is inscribed "*Sacred to the memory of James Evan Fowler who was born at Raddery 15th December 1848 and who died at sea, 17th February 1896.*"

The grave of Eliza and Hugh Junor.
See facing page

Hugh Junor of Essequibo

The Fowlers of Raddery weren't the only family to venture to the West Indies to find fame and fortune. In Rosemarkie Churchyard there stands a stone to the memory of Eliza Junor and her brother William, children of Hugh Junor of Essequibo, British Guiana.

Eliza and William Junor were born in Essequibo, British Guiana (now Guyana). There is no mention of their mother in the local records, but it is assumed that she was either a slave or a free slave. It was common for estate owners to take a slave and have children. Eliza and William appear to have been well cared for by their father.

Hugh Junor from the Black Isle ventured to Guyana sometime in the early 1800s. Attempts to find more information on Hugh, and perhaps to connect him to the many Junors who still live in Rosemarkie and the Black Isle, have sadly, been unsuccessful. However, on Dr David Alston's excellent website, *Slaves and Highlanders*, he writes that "*...in 1815 Hugh, in partnership with Alexander Henderson, bought a timber estate in Essequibo together with its sixty slaves.*"

When persons quit the colony, they had to give notice, and a notice posted in the *Essequibo and Demerara Gazette* for three consecutive weeks in August 1816, stated that Hugh Junor and his daughter Eliza and son William were to quit the colony within the next six weeks.

Eliza and William attended Fortrose Academy. In the Academy records dated 15th December 1818, the visitors and directors of the Academy, together with "*...several gentlemen of the Town and Vicinity, together with the Magistrates of Fortrose and several members of the Presbytery of Chanonry have assembled today for the examination of several classes.*" In the list of prize-winners in the Rector's class, we find the following: "*For Proficiency in Penmanship, Miss Elizabeth Junor from Demerara.*"

On 1st September 1817 Hugh Junor married Martha Matheson, daughter of Colin Matheson of Bennetsfield. They went on to have a son, Colin. Hugh Junor died sometime in 1823 and in 1826 Hugh's widow Martha, married the Reverend Archibald Huowy, minister of St Andrew's Church, Demerara.

Eliza appears next in London where she has given birth to an illegitimate daughter. In the baptismal records of the Parish of St George, Middlesex, Emma MacGregor was baptised by the Reverend W Ducket on 3rd June 1838. Her mother is Eliza Junor and her father is listed as Thomas MacGregor, Gentleman, of Great Hermitage Street, London.

Eliza later moved back to the Black Isle. In the 1851 Census she was living with her aunt Catherine MacKenzie, "*an independent lady*" at 3 Union Street, Fortrose. Her occupation is "*Dressmaker.*" Ten years later she was still living at 3 Union Street and included in the 1861 census form was her daughter Emma MacGregor, Governess, visiting from England. On 17th April 1861, ten days after the compilation of the census, Eliza died at Fortrose aged fifty-seven. There was no medical attendance and the cause of death was unknown. Attempts to track down Emma MacGregor have been unsuccessful.

General Sir Richard O'Connor

General Sir Richard Nugent O'Connor KT GCB DSO & Bar MC ADC came to live in Rosemarkie in 1947 on his retirement from the British Army. His wife Jean was the daughter of George Ross of Cromarty House, and during their married life they made numerous visits to Jean's family in Cromarty, so it was natural that they should choose the area for their retirement.

General O'Connor had a distinguished career in the British Army, in both the First and Second World Wars, so when it came to writing a short biography of his life there was a tremendous amount of information available online. Military archives, unit histories and some of General O'Connor's own private papers provided copious information, as did the excellent biography *The Forgotten Victor*, written by John Baynes, and published in 1989.

Richard Nugent O'Connor was born on 21st August 1889 in the town of Srinagar, in Kashmir, where his father, Major Maurice Nugent O'Connor, was serving with the 87th Royal Irish Fusiliers. Major O'Connor's wife, Miss Lilian Morris, was the daughter of Sir John Morris, KCSI, who served in the Indian Civil Service and became Governor of the Central Provinces. In 1889, Major O'Connor had an accident and had to return to Britain, where he was put on half-pay, and eventually retired from the army in 1894. The O'Connor family moved to the family home at Ballyrock in Ireland.

Richard, known as Dick, was sent to boarding school at Ronbridge Castle preparatory school and then to Wellington College where he was an average student. His housemaster, saying goodbye to Dick at the end of his final term, joked, "*Tell me when you become a General.*" When Dick was promoted to Major-General in 1938, he was one of the youngest Major-Generals in the army at that time and he duly sent the information to his doubting housemaster.

After eighteen months at the Royal Military College, Sandhurst, Dick was gazetted to The Cameronians (Scottish Rifles) in 1909. When the First World War broke out, he became Signal Officer of the 22nd Brigade and received sudden orders to march to Southampton. The regiment embarked for Bruges and on to Ypres, and so began Dick's war service in France.

In February 1915 he was awarded the Military Cross, one of the first recipients of this newly instituted award. He was involved in many operations during 1915, including Neuve Chapelle, Fromelles, Givenchy and the Battle of Loos, where for a time he was reported missing.

In November 1915 he was promoted Captain and Temporary Major and given command of the 7th Division Signal Company where he gained a reputation for his organising ability and success at sorting out confusing situations. Action in the Battle of the Somme in 1916 was followed by the Battles of Arras and Passchendaele.

O'Connor continued to gather awards and rise through the ranks and on 1st June 1917, three months short of his twenty-eighth birthday, he was awarded the DSO, promoted to Temporary Lt Colonel and given command of a battalion. In 1918 he was sent to the Italian Front where he won the Italian Silver Medal of Honour and a bar to his DSO.

Between the wars, O'Connor's career consisted of college courses and foreign postings. According to John Baynes in *The Forgotten Victor*, O'Connor's diary for 1920 describes his experiences on board a troop ship returning from India. To keep fit, he volunteered to work as a stoker in the engine room and he described his fellow stokers as "*good enough fellows.*" He hadn't a good word to say, however, for the chief engineer or for the rest of the ship's officers and when he reached Suez, O'Connor was so disgusted with the ship, he paid for a berth on a P & O liner to Marseilles where he caught a train to Calais and crossed the channel, arriving in London on 16th January 1921.

An appointment as a company commander at the Royal Military College at Sandhurst ended in 1929 when O'Connor returned to regimental duty with the Cameronians and travelled to Egypt. In 1931 the battalion travelled on to India, to Lucknow, that of the famous siege. He spent two and a half years there, enjoying various sports including polo, cricket and hockey.

In 1938, after a spell at the War Office, O'Connor was posted to Palestine in charge of the 7th Infantry Division. The country was in a state of rebellion bordering on anarchy and O'Connor, unhappy with the way things were being run, formed his own plan of campaign and arranged a meeting with the High Commissioner and the Commander in Chief. He obviously impressed these venerable gentlemen, because next day O'Connor was informed that he was being named Governor of Jerusalem. He could now issue orders direct to the city's police and civil administrators. According to Dr Norman MacLean who was minister of the Scots Kirk in Jerusalem during this time, General O'Connor *"…..became a heroic figure to Jew and Arab alike. Before his appointment as Military Governor of the Holy City, no man's life was safe …but in a short time O'Connor worked a miracle."* Dr MacLean goes on to say that O'Connor made *"Jerusalem as safe as Edinburgh."*

In August 1939, the headquarters of the 7th Brigade moved from Jerusalem to Egypt where General O'Connor had the task of assembling the officers to announce the declaration of war with Germany. At 2am next day they moved off to their war station two hundred miles west of Alexandria. Extensive training and organisation were put in place during the period known as "the phoney war" so that when fighting began in earnest, the 7th were well prepared for the long and arduous battles that followed. O'Connor

was known to the Australian forces as *"the little white-haired terrier – because he never lets go."*

It was at the end of the campaign to oust the Italian army from North Africa that General O'Connor turned his attention to the next stage: moving towards Tripoli to tackle the German contingent which had landed there after the defeat of the Italians. O'Connor travelled to Egypt to discuss his campaign plan with General Wavell and was surprised to see that the walls of the Commander-in-Chief's office were devoid of desert maps and had been replaced with ones of Greece. General Wavell listened to General O'Connor's plan and sounded out the War Cabinet in London. But they had already made up their minds: it was Tripoli or Greece and Greece won.

Deeply disappointed by this decision, O'Connor returned to Egypt. His services to the desert campaign were rewarded by his being created a Knight Commander of the Order of the Bath (KCB) and he became Sir Richard. He was appointed GOC-in-Chief British Troops Egypt and he set about improving the defences of Alexandria and the Suez Canal.

On 12th February 1941 Rommel began his probing of British positions, which soon turned into a full-scale advance. The British army was in disarray, being deficient in men, ammunition and signal equipment. O'Connor's successor in the desert appeared not to be coping with the situation and O'Connor was sent to help and advise, with instructions to report to the C-in-C direct. General Wavell and O'Connor met at Advanced Divisional HQ, and on 6th April, a full-scale withdrawal was in progress. The XIII Corps began to travel east.

O'Connor and his fellow officers were among the last to leave and it was dark as they began their journey. They quickly overtook the retreating army and travelled a long stretch where the road was devoid of traffic. At one point O'Connor thought by the position of the moon that they were travelling in the wrong direction, but he was assured by one of his fellow Generals that it was fine as he knew the road. In due course they came upon another convoy of slow moving vehicles and started to overtake them. Coming to a halt in the middle of this convoy, the driver of O'Connor's car alighted to speak to the driver of the second vehicle. Suddenly he found himself confronted by a German soldier carrying a gun. He was marched back to his car where General O'Connor and his fellow officers were quietly dozing. More German soldiers arrived and the whole party was captured.

The three senior officers, Generals O'Connor, Neame and Combe, were sent to a senior officers' camp near Sulmonak, about seventy-five miles east of Rome. O'Connor was very soon planning his escape but didn't think much of his chances, being short of money and civilian clothes. He wrote a letter to the War Office asking for help in the shape of money, clothes and passports and asked to be put in touch with an agent. He managed to pass the letter to an Irishman, Monsignor O'Flaherty, who was part of a visiting delegation from the Vatican.

During the six months that O'Connor spent at the prison, he was far from idle. He took the opportunity to write a long report on his desert campaign and passed it to one of the US attachés who was visiting the prison by hiding it under the lavatory seat.

In September 1941 he was moved to Vincigliata Castle in Florence and by December of that year he began receiving coded messages from the War Office giving advice and information about escaping. He also received money and maps inside the books and games which were sent to him.

O'Connor's first escape attempt failed when he was captured just as he was being hoisted over the wall by two of his fellow prisoners. He was put in solitary confinement for thirty days and his fellow officers got ten days confined to their rooms. He was able to read and exercise during his confinement however, and he appeared to have been well treated by the jailers, although he wasn't allowed to speak to them. He communicated by writing messages on the lid of his mess tin.

The next escape plan was to dig a tunnel. While O'Connor was in solitary confinement, a committee had been formed to decide on the design of the tunnel and work had commenced in his absence. When he returned, O'Connor assumed control of the tunnelling work.

During the six months of construction, plans were made to decide where the escapees would go. O'Connor and a fellow officer decided to walk to Tirano, and make for the Swiss border. Identity cards arrived from the War Office, and in his subsequent report on the escape, O'Connor was full of praise for the ingenuity of the War Office in the way they managed to deliver them. One of the captives also proved himself an excellent tailor and made three suits out of special blanket material, also sent out by the War Office.

The escape through the tunnel was a success and the escapees went their separate ways. Posing as Austrian tourists, O'Connor and his companion were successful in making their way in the direction of the Swiss border. Travelling along a country road, however, they were stopped by two Carabinieri on bicycles. After seven days of freedom, the game was up and they were sent back to Vincigliata where they were locked up in solitary confinement in their rooms for a month.

On 8th September 1943, an armistice was signed between the Allies and Italy and the British POWs were sent by train to Arrezzo where the local Italian garrison was anything but friendly. The day before, the British had been the enemy, now the Germans had taken over that role. O'Connor was in no doubt that if the Germans were to arrive, they would be handed over. The Italians obviously wanted rid of the embarrassing Brits and after two hours at the garrison, they were told they were being provided with two coaches to transport them to a monastery in the Appenines. They appeared to have been freed, but with the country still full of Germans, and with nowhere to go, they decided to keep a low profile. The monks at the monastery were quite pleased to see them and provided them with food and accommodation. However, after a few days, their presence had become known in the vicinity and they were advised to go to another monastery higher up the mountain where it was much more secluded.

O'Connor and his fellow generals then began a hide-and-seek existence in German-occupied territory as they tried to find a way to escape to safety. Eventually they procured the assistance of a trawlerman who agreed to transport the three to the British Zone at a cost of £800, the loan of which was provided by the monastery. They spent an uncomfortable night locked up in the hold of the trawler as a storm raged above. O'Connor was seasick.

The journey was successful, but their troubles were far from over. When they stepped ashore, they were arrested. O'Connor asked to see the officer in charge and when the senior officer arrived, he turned out to be an old colleague of O'Connor and all was well.

A few days later, on Christmas Day 1943, O'Connor landed at Prestwick and was soon reunited with his wife who was with her family at Cromarty. Word quickly spread, however, that O'Connor had been freed, and immediately plans were being made for his return to the war zone. General Montgomery suggested that O'Connor be put in charge of the 8th Army, and after an interview with General Allenbrooke he was given the command. He took up his appointment on 21st January 1944.

In October 1944 O'Connor was so outraged by a decision to sack an American, General Silvester, that on a point of principle he asked to be relieved of his command. He later withdrew his resignation, but this seems to have worked against him and in November 1944 O'Connor was on the move again, being made GOC-in-C Eastern Command with

Sir Richard O'Connor (left), Lord High Commissioner to the General Assembly of the Church of Scotland, with his Chaplain, the Reverend John B Russell, minister of Rosemarkie Parish Church, and Purse Bearer Sir Alastair Blair, Edinburgh, May 1964.

headquarters in Calcutta. It has been suggested that this posting was the equivalent of relieving him of his command.

O'Connor wrote a letter to General Silvester, saying how sorry he was regarding the circumstances of his departure and thanking him for all he had done for his division. This letter was to come back to haunt O'Connor a few years later.

O'Connor wasn't too impressed with Calcutta and when Germany and Japan surrendered the problems of the C-in-C increased. O'Connor found to his disgust that he was now a major political figure, second only to the Viceroy. Despite the political upheavals, O'Connor appears to have enjoyed his time in India. In May 1946 he was told he was being made Adjutant General to the Forces, and by the end of the month he and Jean were on their way back to Britain.

In 1947, Montgomery and O'Connor had a difference of opinion which would eventually drive O'Connor into retirement. Monty was visiting the United States. General Silvester had not forgotten his ignominious sacking a few years earlier, and when a lawyer representing Silvester asked to interview Monty in America, he agreed. The letter O'Connor had written to General Silvester was brought to Monty's attention and it heralded the end of good relations between the two generals. It was a great embarrassment for Monty, especially as General O'Connor refused to withdraw the contents of the letter.

At about the same time, the Army Council agreed to a reduction in the number of infantrymen, but plans which were in place to carry this out were cancelled due to a shortage of transport. O'Connor argued that this was unfair to the men who had been looking forward to demobilisation and said the decision would lead to discontent in the ranks. He was overruled and once again submitted his resignation. This time it was accepted and it caused a rift between himself and Montgomery which lasted for about two years. It was a sad ending to a distinguished military career.

O'Connor was fifty-eight when he left the army in 1947 but it wasn't long before he was drawn back into the army life. In 1948 he was appointed Commandant of the Army Cadet Force in Scotland. This entailed visiting cadet units all over the country, encouraging and offering support.

In January 1951 he became Colonel of the Cameronians (Scottish Rifles) a position he was especially happy to accept. Several other responsibilities came his way. In 1950 he was appointed a Deputy Lieutenant for Ross and Cromarty and in 1952 he became a Justice of the Peace. Then in 1955 he was made Lord Lieutenant for Ross and Cromarty, a position he held until 1964.

While in the position of Lord Lieutenant, Sir Richard was responsible for welcoming HM the Queen and the Duke of Edinburgh on a visit to Cromarty in 1950.

In 1959 Sir Richard was devastated when Jean died of cancer. In 1963, however, he married for a second time. Dorothy Russell was the widow of Brigadier Hugh Russell, Commander of 7th Armoured Brigade during the Western Desert campaign. Dorothy and Jean had been close friends.

Quite soon after the wedding, Sir Richard was appointed by the Queen to the post of Lord High Commissioner to the General Assembly of the Church of Scotland. The post of Commissioner involved ten days of public appearances including attending at least one session of the Assembly each day and four church services. He also visited new churches or church halls, children's homes, old people's homes, hospitals, universities and schools. Several banquets and receptions at Holyrood Palace and a garden party required his attendance. Also, up to ten overnight VIP guests arrived each day and had to be entertained.

Sir Richard's final accolade, and the most prestigious one, came in 1971 when the Queen created him a Knight of the Thistle, an order second only to the Order of the Garter. His installation by the Queen was carried out in the Thistle Chapel adjacent to St Giles Cathedral on 3rd July 1971 and from then on the letters "KT" took precedence over all the other decorations following his name.

The older residents of Rosemarkie remember the modest old gentleman who lived among them for thirty-one years. When the O'Connors moved to Kincurdie, they attended Rosemarkie Parish Church and occupied a pew in the gallery directly opposite the pulpit. At the time, there was a chandelier hanging from the centre of the church and this apparently impeded Sir Richard's view of the minister. Rather than move his seat, Sir Richard arranged to have the chandelier removed.

In 1949 Sir Richard was appointed to represent the Presbytery of Chanonry and Dingwall at the Synod of Ross, Sutherland and Caithness, a position he held until at least 1964.

Sir Richard also took part in many of the local activities, becoming President of the local branch of the Horticultural Society. He presented a silver cup, named The Lady Ross Cup, to be contested annually for the best sweet peas, but, to his extreme embarrassment for the first few years it was won by his own gardener.

He was President of the Fortrose and Rosemarkie Golf Club from 1952 until 1978 and the O'Connor Charities Cup, presented in his memory, is awarded for the four lowest net scores in charity medals.

In the fifties Sir Richard gave several talks to the Rosemarkie Youth Club about his experiences in the two World Wars and of his time as a POW. His talks were illustrated with maps and diagrams and Sir Richard's quiet authority shone through as he described the horrors of war.

Janice MacLeman, who lives in Avoch, has fond memories of Sir Richard O'Connor. Her mother was cook/housekeeper at Kincurdy House from 1953 until the O'Connors moved away in 1978. They lived in the servants' quarters and Janice had limited access to the house, but remembers having regular contact with Sir Richard and his wife.

When she first moved into Kincurdy, Sir Richard taught Janice how to curtsey, *"Just in case you meet royalty."* She never did meet royalty, but she can do a pretty good curtsey should the occasion ever arise. The O'Connors were fond of entertaining and Janice remembers the house always being full of guests, especially when Jean's son visited with his friends. Quite often several boisterous army officers were squeezed into the servants' quarters when the main rooms in the house were full up.

The O'Connors were extremely mindful of the welfare of their staff and Janice recalls that, for many years, her mother suffered from recurring migraines. Sir Richard arranged for her to be examined by a homeopathic doctor in Glasgow. He made all the arrangements and drove Mrs MacKay to Glasgow himself. Everything was paid for by Sir Richard and Mrs MacKay's migraines were cured.

In 1978 the O'Connors left Rosemarkie to live in London and it was there that Sir Richard died on 17th June 1981, two months before his 92nd birthday. He had suffered two strokes which left him paralysed and in a coma. He was buried beside his first wife Jean, in the Old Cemetery at Cromarty House.

Rosemarkie Churchyard

The churchyard in Rosemarkie is far older than its oldest dated stone which, according to the Highland Family History Society record of Monumental Inscriptions, is within the Dunbar Enclosure and is to the memory of Margareta Dunbar and dated 4th December 1644.

In bringing up to date the records of the church in 1815, the Reverend Alexander Wood recorded: "*Andrew Murray, Regent of the Kingdom in reign of David II died 1338 and was buried at Rosemarkie.*"

Sir Andrew Murray (1298-1338) was, according to the Oxford Dictionary of National Biography, the posthumous son of Andrew Murray who died of wounds received at the battle of Stirling Bridge in 1297. By 1320 Murray, who is described as a soldier and administrator, had been knighted. In 1326, already a widower with two sons, Murray went on to marry Christian, sister of Robert I and widow of Sir Christopher Seton. After the death of Donald, Earl of Mar, at Dupplin Moor, Murray was chosen to be Guardian of Scotland during the minority of David II. Active during the long wars of Independence, Murray eventually retired to his castle at Avoch, where he died in 1338. He was buried at Rosemarkie, but his remains were afterwards removed to Dunfermline Abbey.

It is more likely, however, that Sir Andrew was buried in the Cathedral in Fortrose. C G Macdowall, in his book *The Chanonry of Ross*, quotes from *The Orygynal Cronykil of Scotland* by Andrew de Wynton, who recounts the burial of Andrew de Moravia in the "*Kirk Cathedral of Rosemarkie.*"

Mr Macdowall says: "*…for a long period state records and ecclesiastical documents continued to apply the word Rosemarkie to an area larger than the village of that name.*" He goes on to give instances of this, including individuals who described themselves as "*Dean of Rosemarkie*" and "*Treasurer of Rosemarkie*" when they were clearly connected to the Cathedral or to the Episcopal Church of Fortrose. He concludes: "*It seems to be clear therefore, that the name Rosemarkie was not limited to the village…*" but included "*…the peninsula and the lands behind it.*"

The Reverend Robert Findlay, minister in Rosemarkie Church from 1709 until his death in 1733, is buried in Rosemarkie churchyard.

In 1853 the Rev Alexander Wood found that Robert Findlay's gravestone was being eroded and had it renewed at his own expense as he wished to "*…preserve the memory of this important personage.*" Initial attempts to research the Rev Robert Findlay were in vain, apart from finding his marriage details. Closer inspection, however, revealed that far from being a famous person, he appears to be infamous!

According to Macdowall's *The Chanonry of Ross*, a Presbyterian Minister, Mr Robert Findlay was inducted into Rosemarkie Church in 1709. Fortrose didn't have a Presbyterian minister at the time and in 1716 the Presbytery of Chanonry appointed Mr Findlay to preach in Chanonry as well as Rosemarkie. In a short time his sermons were attracting "*…three or four score and often, upwards of a hundred persons.*"

It is not known what went wrong, or who offended Mr Findlay, but his sermons in Fortrose tailed off to about two or three a year. He called the town of Chanonry "Sodom", the people atheists, and said the curse of God was upon the place. In his sermons from the pulpit, Mr Findlay is said to have "*…exposed the Magistrates of the Burgh to the contempt of the inhabitants, weakening their authority and leaving a bad impression on the minds of strangers.*"

At the time of the herring feeding, the town was thronged with strangers and it was feared that Mr Findlay preached with such passion that he exposed himself to laughter and ridicule.

The Rosemarkie Session presented a petition to the Presbytery and the Synod, asking that the minister be "...*liberated from the duty of preaching at Chanonry.*" The Synod asked the General Assembly for funds to support a minister at Chanonry, but without success. The Assembly suggested that Mr Findlay preach at Rosemarkie on Sunday and at Chanonry during the week. The problem seems to have rumbled on for years and had still not been resolved when Mr Findlay died in 1733.

The inhabitants of both Rosemarkie and Fortrose must have breathed a sigh of relief when the Rev John Wood, the first of the Wood dynasty to preach in Rosemarkie, was appointed in 1734.

The gravestone of "The Last Man", Dr William Brydon.

See next pages

Dr William Brydon

Few people know that Rosemarkie Churchyard is the resting place of a remarkable man who served the Empire with distinction. Dr William Brydon's survival in the retreat from Kabul became one of the legends of the Victorian era and his arrival in Jalalabad is depicted in *The Remnants of an Army*, a painting by Lady Butler which hangs in the Tate Gallery.

William Brydon was born in London on 10th October 1811, the second of eight children of William Brydon and his wife Mary Ann Comberbach. He was educated at Bromley in Kent and went on to study medicine at University College, London, and Edinburgh University. He joined the East India Company as an assistant surgeon in October 1835.

The East India Company (EIC) was an English joint-stock market company formed to carry out trade with the East Indies. It traded mainly with the Indian subcontinent, China, the Northwest Frontier area and Baluchistan. In December 1600 it was granted a charter by Queen Elizabeth I, making it one of the oldest trading companies among similar European trading companies operating in the area. The company shares were owned by wealthy merchants and aristocrats, the Government having only indirect control of the company and owning no shares.

The company grew to become one of the most prestigious of its kind, eventually accounting for almost half of the world trade in basic commodities, including cotton, silk, indigo, salt, tea and opium. The birth of the British Empire in India began with the East India Company.

As well as carrying out extensive trading activities, the East India Company formed its own private armies, exercising military power and carrying out administrative functions. Company rule began in 1757 and lasted until just after the Indian Rebellion of 1857, when the Government of India Act 1858 led to the British Crown assuming direct control of India in the form of the British Raj. The East India Company was dissolved in 1874, by which time the official Government of British India had taken over all administrative and military functions.

When William Brydon joined the company, it was still in its ascendancy and there was plenty for the army to do to keep the wheels of the company turning, especially during the regular skirmishes with the native population who found themselves overwhelmed. Brydon spent his time in the north-western provinces of India, attached to various regiments, and in 1839, at the outbreak of the war with Afghanistan, he was posted to the 5th Native Infantry in Kabul.

In January 1842 the garrison, under the command of Major-General William Elphinstone, decided to retreat to Jalalabad, having been promised safe passage for the sixteen-thousand-strong party which included wives and children. Their ten-day journey, through narrow gorges and high passes, was difficult because of deep snow and when the retreating garrison was attacked by Afghan fighters, Brydon and five other British officers were the only survivors.

Brydon and his fellow officers made their way to Fatehabad, four miles from Jalalabad, where his companions were killed and Brydon himself was wounded in the knee and hand. He also received a severe blow to the head from an Afghan knife, only escaping death when the knife was deflected by a copy of *Blackwood's Magazine* placed under his cap for extra warmth. When he eventually reached Jalalabad, he became known as "*the last man.*" When asked where the army was, he is said to have replied, "*I am the army.*"

Dr Brydon, however, was not the only member of the gar-

Remnants of an Army, **1879, by Elizabeth Thompson, Lady Butler,** *© Tate Britain*

rison to survive the retreat. Over a hundred British officers, soldiers, wives and children were taken captive and eventually released by the Afghan tribesmen. Some Indian sepoys who survived the massacre made their way to Jalalabad over the next few weeks. Everybody loves a good story, however, and the myth of "The Last Man" lives on.

William Brydon married Colina Maxwell Macintyre, a sister of Major-General Donald Macintyre VC, in Bareilly,

India, on 10th April 1844, and they went on to have eight children, five of whom were born in India: William on 29th May 1845 in Indore, where his father was Assistant Surgeon attached to the Bhopal Contingent; Margaret Elizabeth born on 1st December 1846 at Mhow, not far from Indore, and Hector John born 2nd September 1848 also at Indore, Bengal. The family had moved by the time Charlotte Sidone was born on 6th September 1850 and was living at Allahabad,

Bengal, where Dr Brydon was Surgeon attached to the 40th Regiment of the British Forces in India. Due to ill health, Dr Brydon returned to the UK on three years' sick leave and this may have been where their fifth child was born. Mary Ann was born in 1854 but there appears to be no record of her birth, either in the UK or in India.

Dr Brydon travelled a great deal with the army, and the ever faithful Colina moved around the country with him. In 1856 she was back in India, living in Calcutta with her daughter Mary Ann, and it was there that her sixth child, Herbert Travers (Bertie) was born on 31st October. Her four elder children had been left behind in the care of relatives in the UK.

In *The Last Man: the life and times of Surgeon Major William Brydon CB* by John Cunningham, Colina Brydon is portrayed as a *"strong, interesting and extraordinarily capable woman, a devoted wife and mother and a stalwart companion in the face of extreme hardship."* This was certainly true. In May 1857 Colina and her two children were living in a bungalow in the army cantonment in Lucknow where her husband was attached to the 71st Native Infantry. Colina kept a diary during this time and *Diary of the Doctor's Lady* was published by Geoffrey Moore, a Member of The Orders and Medals Research Society, in 1958.

On 3rd May 1857 the opening entry in Colina's diary reads: *"Officers summoned from church during the service to quell a mutiny in the 7th Oude Local Infantry at Moorsalebaugh. They were disarmed and all troops returned to their lines by 1 a.m."* The 71st Native Infantry was one of the first native regiments to mutiny and this insurrection was to lead to the infamous Siege of Lucknow.

Colina's diary records the everyday happenings of life in the cantonment and it was obvious they were preparing for the worst. Big guns were brought in and the defences were strengthened. On 19th May, Colina and her two children joined ten or twelve other families in the Governor's house

and, on 20th May, Colina recorded the first casualty.

As news came in daily of uprisings all over the country, Colina recorded them all. When the attention of the mutineers turned to the cantonment at Lucknow, the casualties increased and Colina recorded the attacks, every officer's death and even his injuries. She recorded the hanging of mutineers: one morning two, next day six, another day eight. When spies were caught they were given no mercy.

By 7th June the attacks increased and Colina began to help out with nursing the casualties. The weather was getting hotter and on 23rd June, Colina recorded the first death from cholera. On 29th June she wrote: *"Mrs Haile died of cholera and … Mrs Inglis pronounced to have smallpox."*

On 30th June, a prolonged bombardment took place and there was *"…great confusion and mismanagement."* The native artillery and drivers had deserted, taking with them several guns essential to the defence of the cantonment. Two children died of cholera.

That night an attempt was made to complete a large bastion at a damaged corner of the compound and work continued during the night. Colina recorded: *"The mutineers have completely surrounded us and I fear that our real siege has commenced."*

The siege had indeed begun and work fortifying the compound went on round the clock. The ladies, including Colina, were kept busy supplying the men with tea and brandy. The ladies also helped out regularly at the hospital. Attacks were more frequent, casualties more numerous. Cholera and smallpox were rife. Food was also becoming scarce, especially milk and those who had supplies shared it with families with young children.

During July the fighting became intense and most of the servants at the cantonment had left, so the officers' wives were learning to wash clothes and cook. Colina continued to take her place on watch every night.

On 21st July, Colina had a lucky escape, but Dr Brydon

was shot. Colina recorded the event. *"Oh sad day! Good kind Major Banks shot dead through the temple. I had just finished helping their good nurse prepare him for his good wife to see and had been with her through the sad scene. We were at dinner. I was thankful to leave the table and had gone to the store to see about some wine and there Mrs Apthorpe followed me and told me that my dearest William was hit, shot through the loins."* Dr Brydon, although seriously injured, eventually recovered.

Next day Colina had another lucky escape when a lady walking beside her was struck on the side of the nose by a matchlock ball which penetrated her head. She died in a few seconds in front of Colina.

For a few days both of Colina's children were unwell. Bertie was ailing, getting thinner. She doesn't say what was wrong with him, but we can assume that he was malnourished and might be suffering from a feverish cold with which several children were afflicted. Mary Ann was drooping sadly and had lost her appetite. She kept repeating *"baby so tired,"* which the doctor said was because of a lack of fresh air.

Children were being born and children were dying. The officers' wives took care of the orphans, taking them into their own homes.

In one entry, Colina recorded an execution which might have been a terrible mistake. *"In the morning a man was executed in front of one of our posts and it is feared the poor man was a messenger, had letters and being detected was so punished. We hope not an old pensioner who has been backwards and forwards several times and very faithful."*

All through the months of August and September, Colina recorded the births and deaths of children. On 15th August she wrote: *"So many little children are suffering and sinking."*

In mid-August word came that a relief force was on its way to Lucknow, but when fighting broke out at Cawnpore, the relief force was diverted to protect it. Disappointment reigned.

After the death of the Governor of the cantonment, Sir Henry Lawrence, his belongings were sold by auction. Brandy was selling at a hundred and fifty rupees a dozen bottles, a hundred rupees for half a dozen; beer at sixty rupees a dozen, preserved soup and meats a hundred and fifty rupees a half dozen, macaroni fifty rupees for a small box, and cheapest of all, champagne at fifty rupees. Colina liked to buy small pieces of china and snapped them up when she could. She complained of very high prices at some of these sales, but with food in short supply and their clothes destroyed during the siege, they had to buy what they needed when they could.

On 23rd September a letter was received from Sir James Outram who, with an army of five regiments under his command, was on his way to Lucknow. Spirits were rising. On 24th September heavy firing was heard in the distance and the army was estimated to be about six miles away. That night a commotion was heard in the bazaars of Lucknow, believed to be looting as the rebels prepared to flee. After a second night of looting and firing in the city, the army marched into the cantonment. The siege was over.

On 16th November 1858, the War Office announced that William Brydon Esq., Surgeon of the Bengal Establishment of Her Majesty's Indian Military Forces, was one of several officers made a Companion of the Order of the Bath.

Dr Brydon retired from the army in 1859 and moved to the Black Isle, settling for a time in Meadowbank, Fortrose, the house owned by Colina's mother and where Colina gave birth to their seventh child, Edith Comberbach, in 1860. Dr Brydon acquired the tenancy of Westfield House, Nigg, in the spring of 1861 and it was here that their eighth and last child, Donald MacKenzie, was born in 1866. In 1862, Dr Brydon was appointed honorary surgeon to the 96th Highland Rifle Militia commanded by his close friend Lieutenant Colonel George William Ross of Cromarty.

Dr Brydon died at Nigg on 23rd March 1873 aged sixty-

Rosenberg, Cromarty c1930.

two and was buried in Rosemarkie Churchyard.

After her husband's death, Colina enlisted the help of friends to campaign for an adequate pension, arguing that her husband's premature death was attributable to his long active service and in particular, his wound sustained in the Siege of Lucknow. When his Will was published, Dr Brydon's effects were worth under £200 so Colina was in desperate need of funds. She was granted an annual pension of £100, hardly adequate for a widow and five dependent children. Help was at hand however, when Colina's uncle, Colonel Hector MacKenzie, who had retired to MacKenzie Cottage, Fortrose, bought Rosenberg in Cromarty so that his widowed niece could live there rent-free for the rest of her life. Colina died of old age on 15th December 1899 at Rosenberg.

In his excellent biography of Dr Brydon, *The Last Man,* John Cunningham writes: *"The grave remained without any indication that it was the last resting place of a man who, for one brief moment, captured the attention of an empire and whose sur-* *vival in the retreat from Kabul became one of the legends of the Victorian era."*

The following obituary appeared in *The Invergordon Times* on 9th April 1873. Written by Dr Brydon's friend Colonel Francis Cunningham it gives the last word to "The Last Man." Dr Brydon *"…was a man of modest and retiring ways and much loved by those who knew him well. Under Providence, he owed his marvellous escape to his dauntless heart, his calm self-possession and (not the least important of the three) his extremely light weight. Few soldiers have ever gone through greater perils and you might have been a month in his company without discovering that he had done more than cross the Cromarty Firth."*

Major General Donald Macintyre VC

Within the Macintyre Enclosure on the east side of the churchyard lie several members of the Macintyre family who distinguished themselves in the service of King (and Queen) and Country during the 18th and 19th centuries.

The most famous of these, Donald Macintyre, was born at Kincraig House, Invergordon on 12th September 1831, the second son of Donald Macintyre and his wife Margaret. Donald came from a long line of fighting men. After the Union of 1707, and the subsequent Jacobite rebellions of 1715 and 1745, many Highlanders joined the East India Company with a view to restoring their fortunes, sorely depleted in the decades following Culloden. Lieut. General John Macintyre of the Bengal Artillery, (grandfather of Major General Donald Macintyre VC) appears to be the first of several generations of Macintyres who made the journey to India, arriving there in 1771.

General John's son, Donald Macintyre, (father of Major-General Donald Macintyre VC) became a merchant with the East India Company, with offices in Bengal and London, so for Donald, already with links to India, it was natural that he would follow his father and grandfather to the sub-continent. According to the Forces War Records, Donald was commissioned in 1850 and by 1871 he was serving with the 2nd Gurkha Rifles in the rank of Major, when he was involved in an action that resulted in his being awarded the Victoria Cross. The mountain area to the east of India, bordering Assam, was attracting British tea planters, but their settlement was being resisted by the local tribes, particularly the Nagas and the Lushais.

James Winchester, a plantation overseer at Beckrampore, and a native of Elgin, accompanied by his small daughter Mary, was visiting a fellow-planter, George Sellar, in a neighbouring plantation when they were attacked by a group of

Maj Gen Donald Macintyre VC in his heyday and in later life.

hill tribesmen. In the chase that ensued, George Sellar escaped, but James Winchester, running with Mary on his back, was shot dead. Mary was captured by her pursuers and carried away.

In late 1871, the Bengal government sent an expedition to recover Mary. On 3rd January 1872, the 2nd Gurkha Rifles, under the command of Colonel MacPherson and with Major Donald Macintyre as second-in-command, reached a village called Lal Gnoora where they believed Mary Winchester was being held. They found the village fortified by a 9ft-high bamboo stockade and a heavy smokescreen caused by several fires.

According to the official report on the action, the day was won due to the bravery of two of the men of the 2nd Gurkhas. Under heavy fire from the tribesmen, Major Macintyre and a Gurkha called Inderjit Thapa climbed over the spiked and burning stockade and successfully cut a way through for the rest of the regiment to follow.

For his part in the dramatic rescue of Mary Winchester, Donald Macintyre was awarded the Victoria Cross, mentioned in despatches, promoted to Lt Colonel and received the thanks of the Governor-General. Inderjit Thapa received the Indian Order of Merit, third class. This was the highest order available to Indian/Nepalese soldiers at the time. It wasn't until 1911 that native Gurkhas became eligible to receive the VC, and the first native Gurkha to receive the award was in 1915, during the First World War.

Instituted by Queen Victoria after the outbreak of the Crimean War in 1854, the Victoria Cross is awarded for *"outstanding courage or devotion to duty in the presence of the enemy."* This is the highest award for gallantry in the British armed forces. The medal consists of a cross in bronze with a lion *statant guardant* on the royal crown, with the words *"For Valour"* on a semi-circular scroll. The VC is usually presented to the recipient or to their next of kin by the British Monarch at an investiture held at Buckingham Palace.

Donald Macintyre was a prolific hunter and he travelled extensively in the Himalayas. In 1891 he published a book of his travels, titled *Hindu-Koh: Wanderings and wild sport on and beyond the Himalayas.* He dedicated the book to HRH the Prince of Wales, who was Honorary Colonel of Donald's former Regiment.

Donald usually travelled with Gurkha guides and the book details his journeys and his many kills, so it is not a book for the animal-lover. The slopes of the Himalayan range appear to be thickly forested and are teeming with game: bears, large and small deer, tiger, leopard, wild boar, elephants and many exotic birds.

Donald did, however, have an appreciation of his surroundings and his description of a Himalayan sunrise is worth recording. He describes how the snowy summits flush up with exquisitely beautiful but utterly indescribable

Medals, including the Victoria Cross, awarded to Major General Donald Macintyre.

tints of delicate rose when touched by the first gleam of morning. Gradually the ruddy glow spreads from peak to peak and grows brighter and more yellow, *"...until the whole jagged line becomes suffused with golden light as the sun rises over it in dazzling glory."*

While on a hunt in the high mountains he was distracted on a shoot by the beauty of the rhododendrons which were in full bloom. *"Some were white as snow, others of a salmon red, and ranged from the faintest blush of pink to deepest rose."*

Donald described at one point, while descending steep scree, how difficult it was not to make a noise. He explains: *"...my two companions, with bare feet ... contrive to field the stones set in motion by my heavy nailed boots."* The native stalkers travelled barefoot, but when negotiating steep rocky ground or hard sloping snow, they wore sandals fashioned from twisted ropes of rice straw which they could make in about an hour.

Donald took aim at everything that came within his range, but on one occasion he had cause for regret when he came across two brown bears feeding in a wide gully. He planted a bullet between the shoulders of a large male and the bear was dead. Donald then went in search of its companion. He found the female, together with two cubs, feeding further down the slope and watched them for some time from a distance of about a hundred yards. He wrote: *"As I considered the youngsters quite big enough to take care of themselves, I aimed deliberately at the old lady and let drive; she rolled a short distance down the hill and after a few struggles and grunts, expired."* On seeing their mother lying motionless, the cubs ran down the slope towards her and began grunting and sniffing around their mother for some time, before retiring to a patch of wood *"where they continued their whining lamentations, occasionally venturing out a few yards to stand upright and watch us as we ruthlessly stripped their dam of her hairy coat."* Donald was touched by the behaviour of the cubs and wrote: *"I felt quite sorry I had shot her."*

Donald Macintyre retired from the army on 24th December 1880. On 5th September 1882, he married Angelica Alison Patteson in Kinettles Free Church, Forfar. Her father, the Reverend Thomas James Patteson, officiated. Donald was fifty years of age and Angelica twenty-four.

Major-General Macintyre inherited MacKenzie Lodge in Academy Street, from his uncle Hector MacKenzie. Hector may have built MacKenzie Lodge, although it wasn't always called this. The 1861 Census records show him living in MacKenzie Cottage, a house of eleven rooms. Not exactly a cottage, which may indicate that it was actually what came to be known as MacKenzie Lodge. Hector was sixty years old, unmarried and living there with a domestic servant and a cook, Janet MacKay and Margaret Sutter. He is described as a Colonel in the East India Colonial Service.

Hector MacKenzie died on 31st December 1886 at 9 o'clock in the morning. According to his death certificate, he

MacKenzie Lodge, Academy Street, Fortrose.

was found in a cabin of the steamer Rosehaugh berthed in Fortrose Harbour. He was eighty-three.

In his will, Hector bequeathed the sum of £2,000 to King's College, Aberdeen. According to an article in the *Dundee Courier* dated 10th January 1887, the sum was *"for the foundation of two bursaries for boys of kindred, or of the name of MacKenzie, with a preference in favour of boys belonging to the parish of Rosskeen, the native parish of Colonel MacKenzie, or of the County of Ross."* He also left £500 to the Royal Northern Infirmary, Inverness.

In the 1891 Census, Donald Macintyre and his family were now resident in MacKenzie Cottage, renamed MacKenzie Lodge. He had three children and five servants, among whom were Jessie Matheson, housemaid, and George Scopes, coachman.

On 29th September 1888, a meeting was convened within the Drill Hall, Fortrose, to discuss the formation of a golf club. Although he wasn't present at the initial planning meeting, General Macintyre was appointed to the Council of the new club, no doubt proposed by his brother, General John Macintyre of Meadowbank, who was appointed

Items rescued from MacKenzie Lodge after the fire in 1944.

President.

Donald Macintyre died at MacKenzie Lodge on 15th April 1903 and his wife Angelica on 29th December 1932.

On 10th March 1944, MacKenzie Lodge was accidentally set on fire. Rumour had it that the Norwegians, who were billeted there, had been careless with their cigarettes and had set it alight, but Donald Macintyre's granddaughter-in-law, Ione Tayler, maintained that, according to the family history, a faulty stove was placed too close to the wood panelling in one of the rooms which set it alight. A brief newspaper article about the fire reported that MacKenzie Lodge was being used as a military hospital at that time. This was supported by the late George Taylor, Fortrose, who remembered that after the Norwegians left, MacKenzie Lodge became a naval hospital and it was operating as such when the fire broke out. Naval records have been checked for proof to support this, but without success.

The Fire Brigade had difficulty getting close enough to

MacKenzie Lodge to extinguish the fire, so hundreds of local people formed a human chain to pass buckets of seawater from the seafront, up St Andrews Walk to douse the fire. The house was completely destroyed, with only the contents of the Major-General's study being saved. Stag heads, moose heads, bear heads and other stuffed animals now adorn the walls of MacKenzie Cottage, together with dozens of small water colours and drawings completed by Donald during his time in the Himalayas. MacKenzie Lodge was not rebuilt.

On a lighter note, a few days after the fire, some Fortrose schoolboys, including the late Charles MacLennan of Rosemarkie, got hold of a consignment of condoms and, thinking they were balloons, blew them up and let them loose outside the school.

George and Jessie Scopes

George and Jessie Scopes were valued members of the Macintyre household. When they married they were housed in a cottage in Academy Street, opposite MacKenzie Lodge. According to the Tayler family, descendants of Donald Macintyre, this building was once the stables and was converted by Donald for use by George and Jessie. When Jessie died she was described as *"a faithful servant for many years."*

According to local gossip, Jessie Scopes was the last person to be convicted at the Tolbooth in Fortrose, in 1927. She was accused of public disorder, having had a dispute in the street with one of her neighbours, although this cannot be confirmed as there are no records available for the Tolbooth.

George Scopes was a Cockney who joined the 1st Battalion Rifle Brigade in 1857. He served his time in India where he was batman to Major-General Macintyre who brought him to Fortrose when he retired there. George married Jessie Matheson in Fortrose Free Church on 5th December 1893.

George Scopes took an active role in the life of the Burgh of Fortrose. On Tuesday 5th November 1912, the annual election of Town Councillors took place and George was successfully elected with a total of sixty-seven votes. He was made *"Burgess and Freeman of the Burgh of Fortrose with all the privileges and liberties thereupon appertaining."* George obviously took his role seriously as he was one of the more regular attenders at the council meetings over the years. He served until shortly before his death in 1925, aged sixty-one. George was buried in Fortrose Old Cemetery.

Jessie Scopes.

Mary Winchester

Mary Winchester was seven years old when she was rescued from the Lushais. After a year in captivity, she had learned a few of the tribal habits, one of which was the smoking of a pipe. She was eventually repatriated and lived with her grandparents in Elgin, where she became quite a celebrity.

Mary's rescue was widely reported in the press in the UK, in newspapers ranging from the *Dundee Courier* to the *Buckinghamshire Herald*. One report, in the *Western Daily Press*, Bristol, dated 6th May 1872, is from an unnamed correspondent writing from Elgin. It begins: "*Yesterday I had an interview with the little girl, Mary Winchester, lately released from the Lushais by the Bengal Government.*" The report goes on to say that Mary was reluctant to discuss the people who held her in captivity and when references were made to the Lushais she replied that she didn't want to see or hear of them. According to the correspondent, Mary was well liked by her captors and when the stockade was stormed and the Lushais were about to be routed, they provided Mary with clean clothes and cut off her hair, which by Mary's account was long and beautifully curled, to keep as a souvenir.

Mary was given into the care of a native Gurkha, Captain Scubedar, and the correspondent was shown a photograph of Mary with the captain. She is reported to have said: "*I do love the Scubedar.*"

Mary said that her complexion was quite white when she left her father's tent, but the scorching heat caused it to darken. In the newspaper reports however, Mary is described as "*a dark-skinned girl*". According to Wikipedia, Mary was the illegitimate child of James Winchester and one of his native workers on the plantation at Cachar, in India, but this has not been confirmed.

After Mary returned to Elgin she lived with her grandparents, James and Jane Winchester, at 2 Lossie Wynd. In the 1881 Census Mary is recorded as having been born in India.

Mary married William Innes Howie on 13th August 1887 at St Andrews Presbyterian Church, London. In the 1911 Census, Mary and William have three children: Francis, born c1889; Mary Winchester, born c1897; and Margaret Ogilvy, born 14th August 1898. Mary had kept in touch with her Scottish relatives as her cousin, Hannah Sophia Winchester aged twenty-five, a music student from Stirling, was visiting on the day of the census. Mary died on 18th March 1950 at Southwood Lawn Road, Highgate, London.

Mary Winchester and Captain Scubedar shortly after her rescue from the Lushais.

© *Illustrated London News Ltd/Mary Evans*

The Mackenzies of Flowerburn

Flowerburn House stands a few miles from Rosemarkie and was once part of a much larger estate, encompassing a huge portion of the east side of the Black Isle. The original house was burned down in the 1950s and the present farmhouse is a more modern affair.

The 1891 Census lists the occupants of Flowerburn as Roderick Grogan MacKenzie, his wife, and three daughters: Eva, Alice and Violet. Roderick was serving as a Major, second-in-command, in the Highland Fencers, stationed at Fort George.

Roderick Grogan MacKenzie was the fifth generation of MacKenzies to occupy the Flowerburn estate. When he inherited Flowerburn in 1848 on the death of his father, he was just four years old. However, a Deed of Settlement had been drawn up on 6th September 1848 in which Sir Evan MacKenzie of Kilcoy was appointed curator of the young Roderick.

In January 1860, a company of Ross-shire Rifle Volunteers was formed at Fortrose and the following report appeared in the *Inverness Courier* on 26th January 1860: "*A very numerously attended and enthusiastic meeting of this corps was held within the Royal Hotel, Fortrose on Saturday last (21st) for the purpose of electing the officers and carrying out the other arrangements connected with the full organisation of the Corps.*" It goes on to list the officers in charge, and includes "*Roderick Grogan MacKenzie of Flowerburn to be Ensign.*" An ensign is a standard bearer, the lowest commissioned officer rank. Roderick was aged sixteen.

Roderick had a connection to Ireland through his mother, Harriet Grogan and it may be this connection that persuaded him to join the 16th Lancers in Ireland, in 1863 when he was nineteen years old. The *Southern Reporter and Cork Commercial Courier*, dated 24th September 1863, in its column of appointments, promotions and retirals in the 16th Lancers, reports that: "*…Roderick Grogan MacKenzie to be Cornet by purchase.*" Roderick served for twenty months and when he resigned, in May 1865, he joined the Highland Rifle Militia. In the Army List dated August 1878, Roderick held the rank of Major.

Roderick didn't have far to go to look for a wife. On 22nd February 1872 he married Eva-Mary Marjory Erskine MacKenzie at Belmaduthy House in the parish of Knockbain. Eva-Mary was the daughter of his curator, Sir Evan MacKenzie of Kilcoy.

Eva-Mary doesn't appear to have seen much of her husband in the following years as he climbed the ranks of the Highland Rifle Militia. In the 1881 Census for Ardersier, Roderick and a fellow officer, Alexander Macleay, are seen to be living in lodgings in Ardersier with William and Ann Smith and their seven children. Alexander is the Commander of the Highland Rifle Militia and Roderick is second-in-command.

The Childers Reforms, restructuring the Infantry Regiments of the British Army, were undertaken by the Secretary of State for War, Hugh Childers, in 1881 and brought into effect on 1st July of that year. In this restructuring, the Highland Rifle Militia became part of the Seaforth Highlanders. In the 1891 Census, taken on 5th April 1891, Roderick is a Major in the 3rd Battalion Seaforth Highlanders, living in the barracks at Fort George. Alexander Macleay is also serving in the Battalion in the rank of Colonel.

Roderick Grogan MacKenzie died on 13th October 1892 at Rossclare, Ireland, aged forty-eight, and was buried in Rosemarkie Churchyard. Roderick's eldest daughter, Eva, inherited all of the Flowerburn Estate. On 2nd June 1904, she

Flowerburn House, c1950. Roy Fraser, whose brother Alistair now owns Flowerburn Farm, is the child standing by the car.

married Charles Howard Crosbie, resident magistrate of County Donegal, Ireland, in Kensington, London. Charles appears to have been a bit of a character and he had a colourful past.

An article in the *Royal Cornwall Gazette* dated 21st April 1898 reveals that a Mr Long, a financier of the Strand, London, had taken Charles to court for failing to repay the sum of £192. Charles, an officer in the Irish Militia, claimed he had no assets. In his defence, he said he had borrowed £40 for two months and signed a promissory note for £60. The court took note of the high interest rate (360%) but found in favour of Mr Long.

In the *Royal Cornwall Gazette* dated 18th October 1900, Charles Crosbie was again taken to court, this time for bankruptcy. He failed to attend the court and Judge Granger accused him of disrespect. Apparently Crosbie's London solicitor had made arrangements for the sum to be paid by Crosbie's mother, but had failed to notify the court in advance. The Judge criticised the London solicitors and, as it was not the first time this had happened, said he was setting an example by calling for Crosbie to attend in person and answer the charge of *"disrespect to the court,"* probably the modern-day equivalent of contempt of court. No follow-up can be found to this court appearance.

The Ireland Census of 1911, shows Charles Howard Crosbie, now known as Herries Crosbie, head of the family, to be widowed and living with his daughter, Margaret Carlyle Herries Crosbie, aged six. He had three servants and a companion, Henry Bannie Naunton, single, aged twenty. It is apparent that Eva had died, but there is no trace of her death in the Irish records nor any report of it in the Irish newspapers. With her husband being a magistrate, she might have been worthy of a mention in the press. In the Register of Wills for England and Wales probate calendar, an entry for Eva Crosbie states that she died on 25th October 1907 at Fintra, Killibegs, Donegal.

Charles appears to have established a connection between the Crosbie and Herries families, and in 1907 he changed his name by deed poll to Herries-Crosbie. There is a family tree online which has a direct line of Crosbies, originating with Robert Crosbie of Oulcottis 1415-90. The Herries connection was made when John Crosbie, Provost of Dumfries, married Margaret Herries of Barnbarroch in 1708. In 1921, Charles published a sixteen-page pamphlet entitled *The Story and Pedigree of the Lords Herries of Herries in the Male Line*.

Charles Herries Crosbie joined the 2nd Battalion Cameron Highlanders in 1914 in the rank of 2nd Lieutenant. He transferred to the 6th Battalion in the rank of Captain and towards the end of the war he transferred to the 2/4th Wiltshire Regiment, 2nd Labour Corps, in the rank of Major. The Labour Corps was formed in April 1917 and was manned by officers and other ranks who had been medical-

ly below par, had been wounded or because of their age. Charles would have reached the age of fifty in 1917.

Charles died in Dublin sometime during October/ December 1922 at the age of fifty-four.

When Roderick Grogan MacKenzie's wife, Eva, died on 10th July 1919, Flowerburn was sold. A public roup was held on 30th March 1920. The asking price was £22,250.

Betty Marshall (Elizabeth Sutherland) came to Fortrose in 1946 and she became friendly with the last living daughter of Roderick Grogan MacKenzie of Flowerburn, Alice Maud Harriet, who lived in Flowerburn Cottage, Fortrose. She remembers a lady called Lyle Crosbie coming to Fortrose regularly to visit her aunt, until Alice died in 1950.

Margaret Carlyle Herries Crosbie, daughter of Charles and Eva, and the only grandchild of Roderick Grogan MacKenzie, was the last in the line of the MacKenzies of Flowerburn. She died, unmarried, in Dorset in December 1994 aged 89.

The Grigors of Hopefield

In May 2014, Ann Geddes from Rosemarkie inherited the farm Hopefield, a few miles up the Eathie Road. The house had lain empty and neglected for some years, but underneath the clutter lay a little gem. Instead of being a basic farmhouse, there were large rooms with high ceilings, three period fireplaces, large skirting boards, a beautiful oak staircase and servant bells. Ann wondered if it had been a dower house.

Hopefield Farm was once part of the Flowerburn Estate. When the estate was disposed of in 1920, Bill Grigor and his wife Christine Muir Goodall were the sitting tenants. They purchased the ninety acres for £1,100 and took possession at Martinmas 1920. Bill and Christine's son, Willie, inherited the farm from his father and went on to farm there until his death in 1988. He married Margaret Ross of Ardmeanach in Rosemarkie Parish Church on 11th December 1947.

When Ann Geddes took possession of Hopefield it was full of the possessions of Willie and Margaret. In the sitting room there were two large portraits, plus many old photos and documents which were badly affected by damp.

Ethel Urquhart identified the portraits as her great-grandparents, William Grigor and his wife, Catherine Clark, who farmed at Weston, near Raddery. William and Catherine had nine children, five of whom went on to produce well-known local branches of the family in the area:

(1) Hugh Grigor farmed Balmungie and was the grandfather of Mary, John, Julia (Mrs Chalmers), Hugh and Duncan, some of whom still live in the area. (2) John Grigor was the father of Dahlia Grigor who retired to Fortrose after a career in the ministry. John's son Kenneth was the father-in-law of Jessie (nee MacDonald) and grandfather of Fraser, Lesley and Lindsay. (3) William Grigor (known as Bill) married Christine Muir Goodall, and was the father of Willie Grigor,

Hopefield Farmhouse.

Hopefield. (4) Margaret Grigor married Kenneth Whyte, who farmed near Avoch, and was the grandmother of Maureen, Grigor and George Whyte. (5) Ethel's grandfather was Donald Grigor who married Agnes Cownie. Donald moved away from the Black Isle when he joined the ministry and spent his working life in the south of Scotland. Ethel moved back to the Black Isle when she married Finlay Urquhart from Fortrose. Her sons, Finlay, Kenneth and John, live locally.

Hopefield appears to have been a well-run farm if the transactions carried out over the years are anything to go by. Bill sent animals to the Dingwall Auction Mart, to be sold by Reith and Anderson, almost every week. Sometimes he bought more than he sold. They travelled on the London Midland and Scottish Railway Company line between

William Grigor and Catherine Clark of Weston Farm. Facing page: The wedding of Willie Grigor and Margaret Ross.

Fortrose and Dingwall and transactions were paid in cash.

During WWII, prisoners of war were housed in a hostel in Munlochy and were allowed to work as labourers on farms in the area. The Grigors took advantage of this. According to receipts from the Agricultural Executive Committee for Ross and Cromarty, prisoners were employed at Hopefield from November 1943 until May 1946. The going rate was one shilling an hour paid to the Agricultural Executive Committee. The men worked from November to March each year and the hours varied. Bill and Willie employed one man most of the time. During November each year the number varied from three to five. They also employed soldiers on the farm during November 1945 and November 1946. They were paid one shilling and threepence an hour.

For many years, Willie and Margaret travelled round Fortrose and Rosemarkie, selling their eggs. When Willie died in 1988, Margaret lived alone in the house and was often seen walking to Rosemarkie for her shopping. Locals who knew her always gave her a lift. Eventually Margaret became unable to look after herself properly and she moved into Abbeyfield House, Rosemarkie, where she died in 2014, aged ninety-two.

David Frazer Gordon

The Church played a leading role in providing universal education in Scotland, and in 1859 a vacancy for a schoolmaster arose at Rosemarkie Parochial School. The vacancy was advertised in the *Inverness Advertiser* and from the pulpit of Rosemarkie Parish Church in the summer of that year.

On 31st October, the Reverend Alexander Wood recorded: *"Sir James Randal MacKenzie of Scatwell proposed Mr David Frazer Gordon, at present teacher to the Dumfries Education Society as a proper person to fill the vacant situation and the nomination was seconded by the Reverend Alexander Wood."* Mr Gordon took up his duties immediately.

In the 1861 census, David Gordon and his wife Isabella Baxter, together with their two-year-old daughter Jessie, are resident in the High Street, Rosemarkie. Between 1859 and 1869 Isabella gave birth to seven children: Janet (also recorded as Jessie) born in Dumfries, 1859; a male child unnamed, born in Rosemarkie on 21st December 1860 who presumably died at birth; Mary born 15th May 1862; Robert Henderson born 17th October 1863; Isabella born 25th August 1865; Allan born 24th July 1867; and a female child, unnamed, born 31st March 1869 who again, presumably, died at birth. Isabella's death is commemorated on the family gravestone in Rosemarkie Churchyard as having occurred on 19th April 1869 aged thirty-three years, nineteen days after the birth of her last child.

Poor Isabella hadn't much success with the rest of her family either. Of her remaining children, her daughter Jessie died on 20th March 1866 aged eight years, and Allan died 6th May 1870 aged two years and ten months.

Only three of her children survived into adulthood. In the 1871 Census, Mary, Robert Henderson and Isabella are living with their father and his new wife, Jane, in the High Street, Rosemarkie. Ten years later, only Mary and Isabella are living there, together with four new siblings. Robert has moved to Glasgow and he appears on the 1881 census, living with his aunt and uncle, Alexander and Mary Dryden at 17 Anderson Street, Partick, Glasgow. Aged seventeen, he gives his occupation as an Apprentice Druggist.

In the 1891 Census, Robert, Mary and Isabella are all living together at 11 Muirpark Gardens, Govan. Robert, the head of the household, gives his occupation as a Registered Chemist. Mary is employed as a Clerk, and Isabella, a Housekeeper. Mary was the grandmother of Kathleen MacKay (nee Shannon) who now lives in Dingwall.

Mary went on to marry Gavin Shannon, a journalist, at Partickhill on 12th June 1896. Gavin was aged thirty-six, Mary thirty-four, and they had three children, the youngest of whom, Andrew, was the father of Kathleen. No further trace could be found of Isabella, and Kathleen only remembers Robert coming to visit her family.

It was usual for people in authority to take on certain positions in the community and at a meeting on 22nd August 1863 David Gordon, *"...teacher in Rosemarkie School was unanimously elected clerk to the Rosemarkie Kirk Session at a salary of £2 sterling per annum, to be paid annually at the term of Whitsunday."* He then became an elder of the kirk on 21st November 1867 and Treasurer on 30th March 1868. He was a busy man.

David Gordon's second marriage to Jane, eldest daughter of the late Alexander Fearn, farmer, was publicised in the *John O'Groat Journal* of 12th May 1870. David and Jane were married at 15 Union Street, Nairn on 2nd May, just four days before the death of David's son Allan.

An article in the *Inverness Advertiser* dated 19th November 1880, reveals that Mr D F Gordon had raised an action in the Court of Session against the School Board for non-payment

The Old School, Courthill Road, Rosemarkie. This is a modern photo of the building. It was built sometime in the early 1860s and closed in 1932.

of salary. The Education Scotland Act had by this time come into force and education was compulsory for all children up to the age of thirteen years. David's terms of employment had changed and it would appear that the agreed increase in salary had not been paid to him for several years. The Education Authority abandoned their case half way through the court proceedings and paid up.

David Gordon died on 28th September 1882 leaving Jane with four children under ten years of age. Jane died at Platcock, Fortrose on 4th April 1908 aged sixty-four.

John Carpenter Steavenson

According to local information, John Carpenter Steavenson was responsible for building the house and shop in the High Street, Rosemarkie, now known as Doric House.

Born in Berwick on Tweed on 6th August 1795, John married Elizabeth Fenwick in September 1826. On the marriage certificate, John's address is given as Rosemarkie, so he was already resident here.

John Steavenson, father of John Carpenter Steavenson, was a fish curer based in Fortrose. He was the owner of the sloop *Ann* which was originally built as a fishing boat at Cromarty in 1819 by Alexander Bain, shipbuilder.

In 1822, the *Ann* was broken up, rebuilt and enlarged at Fortrose by John Steavenson. The original keel and part of the timbers were re-used. The *Ann* was registered on 23rd July 1822 at the Port of Inverness, as a vessel which *"….was never before registered."* She was certified as British-built, one deck, one mast, thirty-nine feet in length, twelve feet, four inches in breadth and the depth of her hold was five feet. She weighed twenty-one tons.

The register has no other information on the *Ann*, so it is not known where she plied her trade or what happened to her.

According to Alistair Fraser in his *Random Notes of Old Rosemarkie*, John Carpenter Steavenson leased salmon fishings in Rosemarkie and in the Cromarty Firth and employed a number of men. He was also responsible for building a garden at Ardmeanach, surrounded by a large wall, and spent a great deal of money transporting cartloads of soil at one shilling a load. The Forestry Commission used the garden as a nursery in the 1950s, but it appears now to be abandoned.

John wasn't all that successful as a merchant, as the *London Gazette*, dated 1st October 1830, listed in the Declaration of Insolvency, John Carpenter Steavenson of Fortrose, now of Billingsgate. In January 1832 the *Inverness Courier* carried an advertisement for the sale of his house and garden ground in Rosemarkie at the reduced price of £550.

On 15th September 1837 John Carpenter Steavenson attended a meeting of the Fortrose Town Council where a vacancy had occurred due to the resignation of the Provost, George Tulloch, who had resigned for *"reasons of a political nature."*

George Gillanders proposed that *"…John Carpenter Steavenson Esq, Rosemarkie to be Councillor (interim) in place of Provost Tulloch, resigned."* A secret ballot was then held and John Carpenter Steavenson was unanimously elected Councillor and Provost.

Mr Steavenson's attendance record reveals that he attended only one in three meetings of the council and at the regular election on 9th November 1837 John Stirling was elected Provost. There is no sign of J C Steavenson serving as a councillor from then on, so his stint on the Town Council was short-lived to say the least.

On Friday 18th April 1834 a public roup was held in MacKenzie's Hotel, Dingwall, of the sequestrated estate of JC Steavenson for the sum of £187.10.00, which was the balance due on a loan of £1,500 *"secured by a disposition in security over the Friar's fishing on the River Ness."* There are no buyers and on 30th August of the same year the price was reduced to £20. The buyer was a Mr Stewart of London, but there appears to have been some sort of debenture system in place as on the death of Mr Stewart the fishing rights reverted to the family of JC Steavenson.

John's wife Elizabeth remained in Fortrose during this upheaval, however, as three of her children were born there between the years of 1827 and 1835.

John Carpenter Steavenson died at Birkenhead, Cheshire, on 5th November 1867 aged seventy-two. His death certificate gave the cause of death as *"Died by the visitation of God from natural causes."* It sounds as if his was a sudden death, as the informant was the Coroner for South Cheshire, who had held an inquest into the circumstances.

John Carpenter Steavenson.

George Gillanders

George Gillanders was a well-known member of the community, Provost of Fortrose and Inspector of the Poor for many years and is still talked about by the older inhabitants of Rosemarkie and Fortrose.

George was born in Stornoway in 1805 to George Gillanders. His mother's name is not mentioned in the record of his birth. It's not known when George came to Rosemarkie, but local knowledge is that he came to work for John Carpenter Steavenson in his shop in the High Street in the early 1820s.

George went into business on his own account as an advertisement in the *Inverness Courier* in 1826 reports:

BLACK ISLE WAREHOUSE George Gillanders respectfully begs leave to intimate to the inhabitants of Fortrose, Rosemarkie and their vicinities, that he has lately commenced business in the grocery, hardware and haberdashery lines at Rosemarkie in the shop and premises occupied for some time by Mr James Davidson of Birmingham. As he has purchased all this (sic) *goods at the first markets, with ready money, and under every possible advantage, he feels confident of being able to sell at considerably reduced prices and by a strict attention to business, he hopes to merit a share of public patronage.*

Exactly where George's store was situated seems to be unknown, but there may well have been a shop at the shore of Rosemarkie. He would now be in competition with his old boss John Carpenter Steavenson, who, according to the *London Gazette* of 1st October 1830, was declared bankrupt that year.

On 17th January, 1829, George married Sophia MacKid at Rosemarkie. Sophia came from an interesting family. Her father, Robert MacKid, practised as a solicitor in Fortrose before becoming Sheriff Substitute of Sutherland. It was while he was in this position in 1816, that he was responsible for bringing Patrick Sellar, Factor to the Marchioness and Marquis of Stafford, to court in Inverness on a charge of having *"wilfully set fire to a house of a tinker in Strathnaver and demolishing a mill,"* all part of what has been subsequently termed The Sutherland Clearances.

Patrick Seller was acquitted at the court in Inverness and the reputation of Robert MacKid was sullied to such an extent that he resigned from his post as Sheriff Substitute and moved to Thurso, eventually returning to Fortrose.

Research at the Highland Archives brought to light a document dated 19th January 1830, written by Robert MacKid, acting as Respondent's Agent regarding a petition for sequestration of the estate of George Gillanders. Robert MacKid's appeal for the case to be dismissed is set out in fifteen pages of argument, stating that the citation *"…does not contain a concise and accurate state of fact"*. He says that *"…it does not set out in explicit terms, the nature and grounds for complaint"* and calls the action *"…incompetent and amateurish, raised on the say of an incompetent judge"*. Reading through the long list of reasons for the *"…irregular and illegal petition that ought immediately to be recalled…"* it is clear that Robert MacKid, acting for his son-in-law, was not afraid to speak his mind. Unfortunately there is no documentation to tell us if the petition was recalled, but it is possible that it was, as George continued in business in Rosemarkie.

In 1830 George was elected Baillie in Fortrose Town Council. He was elected Provost on 4th November 1842 and served for almost three years. In October 1845 George tendered his resignation as Provost, to enable him to accept various appointments offered to him under the Poor Law Act, and he became Inspector of the Poor for the parishes of Rosemarkie, Resolis, Knockbain, Avoch and Urquhart/Ferintosh. He continued as a Baillie, however, until he retired from the Town Council in 1856.

According to the 1841 Census, George and Sophia were living in the High Street, Rosemarkie. George gave his occupation as Merchant and he and Sophia now had five children ranging from eight years to eight months. His father-in-law Robert MacKid, aged seventy, was also living there.

George appears to have opened a second shop in Fortrose but may have been a bit ambitious in his business dealings. On 26th May 1841, a notice in the *Inverness Courier* states: *"Valuable Stock of Goods for Sale by private bargain at Fortrose and Rosemarkie. The whole stock of goods belonging to the sequestered estate of George Gillanders, Merchant in Fortrose, in the shops lately occupied by him in Fortrose and Rosemarkie, is now for sale, by Private Bargain in one lot."*

George had a finger in many pies. In 1831 he was appointed Agent for the Militia Insurance Company. One of the jobs of the insurance agent appears to have been to take possession of any wrecks that might occur off the coast and to recover the cost of the contents for his employer.

The following advertisement appeared in the *Inverness Courier*: *"To be sold by public auction on behoof of the Underwriters at Rosemarkie on Tuesday 21st January 1834, the sails, rigging, spars, anchors and cables of the sloop Thames of Banff lately wrecked on the Shore of Rosemarkie. Application to Mr G Gillanders, Merchant in Rosemarkie who is in charge of the wreck."*

A second advertisement in 1843 was for a Public Roup for a cargo of lime landed on the beach at Rosemarkie from the schooner *Frances and Margaret of Newcastle*. Once again, George Gillanders was in charge.

George was also Secretary to the Black Isle Farmers' Society from 1836 to 1841 and again from 1852 to 1873, and in 1849 he was elected to the committee of the North of Scotland Steam Packet Company (Black Isle).

In December 1849 an attempt was made by the Reverend Simon Fraser, minister of the Free Church in Fortrose, to have George Gillanders sacked from his post with the Parochial Board of Rosemarkie on the grounds that he held too many similar offices in the parishes of the Black Isle. There were twenty-three members of the Parochial Board present at the meeting, but the Rev Fraser was unable to find a seconder for his proposal.

Chairman of the Board, Mr MacKenzie of Flowerburn, said that no charges had been brought against Mr Gillanders. He pointed out that the Board approved of the work Mr Gillanders was doing as Inspector and Collector and he proposed a vote of confidence. This was seconded by Mr MacLean of Hawkhill and the motion was carried, 22-1.

A letter of support from the Reverend Miller of Kincurdy was read out. He said it would be a serious loss to the Parish should it be deprived of George Gillanders' services. Mr MacKenzie then warned that the Reverend Fraser should be aware lest *"the strong language and obvious persecution against George Gillanders might not be imputed to a spirit of revenge for the part Mr Gillanders had taken as to Mr Fraser's removal from the Quoad Sacra Church in Fortrose rather than public spirit."* Undaunted, Mr Fraser went on to present a petition, containing fifty-five names, against the erection of a Poor House in the Black Isle for which Mr Gillanders had been campaigning.

In 1854, George Gillanders was the secretary to The Black Isle Union, a committee set up to build a poorhouse to house the poor of all the parishes of the Black Isle. An advertisement was placed in the *Inverness Courier* of 20th July 1854: *"Site wanted either to purchase or feu of not less than two acres of ground for the Black Isle Union Poorhouse. One in the vicinity of any of the towns or villages will be preferred."*

George worked tirelessly for the building of the poorhouse and in 1859 the Black Isle Combination Poorhouse was opened at the Ness, Fortrose.

George was still carrying on a punishing schedule. He

became Secretary to the Directors of Fortrose Academy and in October 1864 he was writing to the Provost of Fortrose Town Council asking the Town Councillors to donate fifty guineas to Fortrose Academy which *"would entitle them to give a voice in the Direction in perpetuity to the Provost or the Magistrates of the Burgh…"* and asking them to discuss this at their next meeting.

George Gillanders attended his last meeting of the Parochial Board on 15th August 1874. He died six days later, on 21st August. A special meeting of the Parochial Board was convened in Rosemarkie Church on 14th September at noon to *"…appoint an Inspector of Poor and Collector of Poor Rates in place of Mr W G Gillanders, deceased."*

At the meeting, George's son, Robert Joseph Gillanders, who was employed as the Town Chamberlain, was appointed to the post of Inspector at a salary of £35. He was also appointed Collector of rates, including the Poor Rates, for the parish of Rosemarkie, plus Registrar of Births and Education, at an annual salary of £30. Robert continued in this role until November 1904 when he retired. His son, William Watt Gillanders, was appointed Assistant Inspector and Collector in July 1904, then became Collector in 1906, and Inspector of Poor in July 1909, following in the footsteps of his father and grandfather. Theirs was another family with three generations of service in Rosemarkie.

Courthill, which was built in 1905 for Miss Mary MacDonald.
See facing page

Jean Baird Villiers

Jean Villiers was a well-known lady who lived in Courthill, Courthill Road, for many years. She belonged to an interesting family with aristocratic connections.

Courthill was built in 1905 for Miss Mary MacDonald, a lady of independent means. According to the 1911 Census, Mary and her sister Mona, a music teacher, were living in Courthill. They are probably the two ladies in the photograph.

Mary's great-nephew, George Frederick Montagu Villiers, inherited the house in 1934 and moved his family to Rosemarkie, prior to his death in July that same year. He left a widow, Mary, and daughters Jean, aged 25, and Constance, aged 21.

George was born at Closeleum Hall, Closeburn, Dumfries-shire in 1871 to Frederick Villiers, landowner, and his wife Jane, a landowner in her own right. George's ancestry can be traced back to Thomas Villiers, Earl of Clarendon, 1753-1824. On the night the 1871 Census was taken, the family members included George's aunt, Viscountess Charlotte Cole, who was visiting. The household consisted of sixteen servants: one cook, two footmen, a valet, a nurse, two lady's-maids, one kitchen-maid, two laundry-maids, two scullery-maids and three house-maids. There was also Henrietta Lupp, aged 23, whose occupation is shown as "Nutman".

Jean Villiers, who outlived all her family, was disabled from birth when the umbilical cord was twisted round her neck and her brain was starved of oxygen. Her family didn't think there was any point in educating their disabled daughter, and it was only when Bernice Smith (nee Junor) went to work as a cook at Courthill, that Jean learned to read. Under Bernice's tuition in the kitchen, Jean was able to master short stories.

When her mother died in 1949, Jean was looked after by a Trust, one of the Trustees being Betty Marshall, Rosemarkie. Florrie Matheson was employed as a full-time companion/housekeeper and a different person was organised for each day of the week, to take Jean out. Betty Marshall took her for picnics. Jean also played golf, badly, but this didn't deter her, and she sometimes won the monthly competition. She was active in St Andrew's Episcopal Church in Fortrose and a regular attender at services. Attending sales of work and stocking up on Christmas and birthday presents, was also something she enjoyed.

Jean was a very popular and much-loved lady in Fortrose and Rosemarkie, but as she got older, it became more difficult to find suitable housekeepers. Courthill was sold in 1974 and Jean moved to a nursing home in Hawick where she died in 1980 aged 71.

George Sutherland

George Sutherland was a prominent Rosemarkie businessman who owned or occupied two meal mills in Rosemarkie: in Bridge Street and at Ootsey, now known as The Old Mill. According to local knowledge, he was the man who built Seafield, the house next to the Plough Inn on Mill Road.

George Sutherland was born on Christmas Day 1841 in Edinkillie, Moray, to William Sutherland and Janet (or Jessie) Sim. George was the fifth child (first son) in a family of eight children. By the 1851 Census, the family had moved to Rosemarkie where William's occupation is miller.

In 1861 George was still living in Rosemarkie. His father, William, had died and George was living in the Rosemarkie Corn Mill, Bridge Street, with his mother and five siblings. He is described in the Census as a miller.

At the age of twenty-two, George found himself in financial trouble. On 20th January 1864, the *Caledonian Mercury* reported that George Sutherland, presently a prisoner in Dingwall, was to be examined in the Courthouse, Dingwall on 20th February for bankruptcy. He had given notice of Cessio Bonorum, which means the relinquishing of property for the benefit of creditors to avoid prison. No further reports on the case could be found, but presumably George was released pending the hearing.

Sometime after 1864 George travelled to Port Canning in the East Indies, no doubt hoping to replenish the coffers after his bankruptcy case. A search for his name on passenger lists of ships heading to and from Port Canning met with no success.

In April 1870 an advertisement in the local press offered *"a mill and miller's house to let at Rosemarkie. Apply to the factor for Flowerburn (Mr Grant, Banker)."* Failing to find a tenant, the Flowerburn Estate sold the land and buildings in 1871 to George Sutherland *"of Port Canning, East Indies, presently*

George Sutherland.

residing in Rosemarkie" for £500. This refers to the mill at the shore sometimes known as Ootsey.

George next appears in the 1871 Census where he was living with his mother Jessie, three brothers and a nephew in Spencer House, High Street, Rosemarkie, a house with five rooms. George described his occupation as *"in East India Rice Trades Corp"*.

The mill on the shore changed hands in 1893 and the new owner, Mrs Mary Ellen Forsyth, named the property *Shandon*. In 1894 it was signed over to a Mrs Buchanan, who sold the property in 1908 to John Sutherland.

On 4th November 1890 George Sutherland was elected Chief Magistrate of the Burgh of Fortrose and on 20th March 1895 he was elected Provost of Burgh (interim) until elections in November of the same year.

In 1902 George was again in financial trouble. In partnership with William Sutherland Chisholm, iron and steel merchant, Glasgow, he brought an action in the Court of Session against the Highland Railway Company, Inverness, regarding a contract between the Highland Railway and Chisholm and Company, Inverness.

By the contract, dated February 1900, Chisholm and Company agreed to build a light railway between the Mound Station and Dornoch. The company began operations under the contract and carried out part of the work. They were sequestrated in November 1900 and the trustees in the sequestration decided not to complete the contract. The arbiters refused to allow George Sutherland and William Sutherland Chisholm to take over the contract and authorised the Highland Railway Company to re-tender for the unfinished work.

In the arbitration, the railway company claimed the sum of £3,908.8.9, which was the difference between the new contract price and the original contract price, and £1,820, as "liquid penalty". George Sutherland and William Sutherland Chisholm declined to appear at the arbitration hearing and in their absence the arbiter found in favour of the Highland Railway Company.

The *Aberdeen Journal* of 4th July 1902 reported that Lord Kincairney, in the Court of Session, was informed that a settlement had been agreed between the Highland Railway and George Sutherland and William Sutherland Chisholm.

George would again be in need of funds to pay his portion of the settlement, and this might have been when he travelled to South Africa. Passenger lists of ships leaving the UK for South Africa, reveal three journeys made by a G Sutherland, single, male, travelling from Southampton to the Cape: 23rd July 1904, 13th April 1907 and 11th December 1909, but it is impossible to confirm that any one of them was George from Rosemarkie.

George died in South Africa on 30th May 1910.

John Sutherland

It was difficult to identify which John Sutherland bought the mill at the shore of Rosemarkie. Jessie Sim gave birth to a son, John, on 18th April 1852, just three months before the death of her husband, William Sutherland.

A second John Sutherland was born into the family. On 6th January 1863, Mary Noble of Learnie gave birth to a son called John. The father is listed as William Sutherland, second son of William and Jessie and a brother of George. Both William and Mary are signatories to the registration.

In the 1881 Census, George's brother John, aged twenty-eight and unmarried, gave his occupation as a farm servant, so it would appear that he was no longer in the milling business.

John the nephew is shown in the 1891 Census to be aged twenty-seven and living with his grandmother Jessie Sutherland and his uncle George in High Street, Rosemarkie. Margaret MacDonald, twenty-one, was a servant in the household. On 1st December 1893, John Sutherland and Margaret, daughter of James MacDonald, Crofter, Conon, were married by special warrant of the Sheriff Substitute of Inverness.

It would appear that Margaret had given birth to an illegitimate daughter, Jane, in 1886, in Conon. Jane is included in the Census return of 1901 when she lived in the Mill House in Bridge Street, Rosemarkie, with John and Margaret. Eight years later, on 27th April 1909, Jane (shown as Jeannie) died at the Mill aged twenty-three. In the 1911 Census, John and Margaret are still living in Bridge Street and they have an adopted daughter, Elizabeth, aged six.

John bought the mill at the shore at a public roup on 5th November 1908 where he was the only bidder. For £50 John received *"the land together with the steam mills and other erections now thereon and whole machinery therein"* This is when the name changed to Ootsey. In the 1915 Valuation Roll, John is shown to be the tenant of the Bridge Street mill. He is also the owner of the *"Mill used as Laundry,"* Shore, Rosemarkie, tenanted by John Robb. It is not known when milling stopped at Ootsey.

The laundry was in business during the First World War and held contracts from several military and naval establishments around the Moray Firth. The sheets and blankets were rinsed in the mill wheel at the burn and laid out to dry on the grass at the shore.

In October 1917 a serious fire occurred in the laundry. The *Aberdeen Journal* of 30th October 1917, reported: *"A serious fire broke out in the Sea View Laundry, Rosemarkie tenanted by Mr John Robb of the Plough Inn, Rosemarkie on Friday evening. The origin of the fire was from an overheating of the apparatus. A lot of clothing and bedding was destroyed but most of the machinery was preserved."*

By 1920, John Sutherland was no longer the owner/occupier of the Mill in Bridge Street. John sold Ootsey in 1918 to John Robb, for £250 and moved to Glenurquhart, Inverness-shire, where he died on 9th November 1951 aged 88.

This photo has been loaned by Grace MacKenzie of Fortrose. It was taken in 1917 and is of the staff of what at the time was called Sea View Laundry, although close inspection reveals "Rosemarkie Laundry" carved into the stone at the extreme right of the photo, behind the head of the man with the white apron. Presumably the gentleman on the extreme left hand side is John Robb, although no-one can verify this. On the back row, third left is Annie Davidson, known as Nando, and fourth left is Molly MacAskill. Fifth left is Jessie Jean Patience, while next to her is Janet Reid (Mrs Patience), mother of Isobel, Jean and Catherine Patience of Avoch. Seventh left is J MacLeman. In the middle row, second left is Janet Patience (Cent) and extreme right is J Patience. Front row second left is Annie Ralph. It has been suggested that the lady third from the right in the front row is a MacIver, but no-one can confirm this.

Rod Anderson

Rod Anderson was a well-known gentleman who is fondly remembered by many of the present day residents of Rosemarkie and Fortrose.

Roderick Anderson was born at the Ness on 17th October 1889, the second child and eldest son of Alexander Anderson, farmer, and Mary Junor.

When he was eight years old, Rod was playing with his friends in the farmyard. He'd been warned not to play on a rusty old plough that was lying there but, boys being boys, ignored the instruction. Rod fell on the plough and cut his leg. He was too scared to tell his parents what had happened and when he eventually did admit to his accident, infection had set in. Dr Cameron, Fortrose, was sent for but the infection was too far advanced and there was no alternative but to have the leg amputated.

All the children from the Ness attended Rosemarkie School but, because it was a shorter distance for him to walk, the young Rod went to Fortrose School. The loss of his leg obviously didn't deter him from taking part in many sporting activities and he won the sack race in the Fortrose School Sports. He also played in goal for the Fortrose Football team.

Rod served his time as a tailor with Campbell's of Beauly and this is where he met his wife, Ann Rebecca MacRae. They were married on 29th April 1915 at Inverness. Rod and Ann Rebecca lived in Beauly for some time, and this is where their daughter Caroline was born in 1916. By the time Mary was born, in 1918, they were living in Rosemarkie, probably in the house at the top of the High Street. A son, John, was born in 1922 and a daughter, Rhoda, in 1926.

Rod was working as a tailor with Kenneth MacRae in Craigbank, Bridge Street, during the Second World War when the building was accidentally burned down. Being out of a job, Rod set up his own business in a shed at the rear of his house in the High Street. He worked by the light of a paraffin lamp for a few years until electricity was installed.

On 4th January 1941, Rod was appointed as an Air Raid Warden by Ross and Cromarty County Council. During the 1950s he was a Trustee of the Gordon Memorial Hall. The Chairman of the committee was the Provost of the Burgh, and the Secretary and Treasurer was Mr WAH Rowat of Rosemarkie.

Anne MacIver remembers her grandfather well and has fond memories of accompanying him to visit his clients in Fortrose. One of Rod's regular clients was Mrs Fletcher from Rosehaugh. For many years Rod was responsible for making all her suits. Mrs Fletcher usually arrived at the cottage in Rosemarkie in a chauffeur-driven car, accompanied by her two dogs. Anne remembers a very grand lady dressed in furs and always wearing a hat.

On one occasion there was enough Harris Tweed material left over from one of Mrs Fletcher's suits to make a pleated skirt for Anne. It was bright pink. Ann hated the colour, but not as much as she hated the hard scratchy material and was glad when she grew out of the skirt.

One of Rod's hobbies was photography and he recorded the many changing scenes of Rosemarkie and Fortrose, building up a sizeable collection over the years. Unfortunately, the collection was destroyed by his son after the death of Mrs Anderson in 1985.

Rod was a regular attender at the numerous whist drives that were held in Fortrose during the winter months. He may also have played bowls but this can't be confirmed. There are conflicting opinions as to what the group in the following photograph are up to. The group would meet up on a Saturday night at the corner of the High Street and Station Road and repair to the back room of the Tavern for a

Back row, from left: Derek MacIver, James Gow; middle row: George MacKenzie, Bill MacIver, Alasdair MacIver; front row: George MacIver, Rod Anderson, Danny Anderson. The fourth person may be Johnny MacIver, but no-one is sure. Derek, Bill and Alasdair were brothers and George was a cousin.

drink or two before the start of the evening's activities. His companions were not averse to a wee dram, but Rod was strictly teetotal and always had a soft drink.

Rod was a regular golfer with a handicap of between 12 and 14 and was a member of Fortrose and Rosemarkie Golf Club for over fifty years. When he ceased playing, he was made an honorary member. On his death, his grand-daughter Anne MacIver donated *The Rod Anderson Memorial Cup* to the club to be contested each year for 3-ball best-ball competition among teams of club members.

Rod Anderson and his brother-in-law George Fraser.

Sergeant James Henderson

Police Constable James Henderson taken when he joined Ross and Cromarty Constabulary in January 1902.

Born 1880 in Kincardine, Ross and Cromarty, James Alexander Evander Matheson Henderson joined Ross and Cromarty Constabulary on 14th January 1902 as a Constable Third Class and was posted to Dingwall. James climbed the promotion ladder quickly and by June 1904 he had reached the rank of Constable First Class. He moved from Dingwall to Stornoway, Tain, Kessock and to Muir of Ord, where he was promoted to Sergeant in October 1909. He also passed an exam to become an Inspector of Weights and Measures, a function he performed throughout the counties of Ross and Cromarty and Sutherland and which he continued after his retirement from the Police.

In 1911 James was transferred to Muir of Ord which was becoming busy and was considered a more appropriate location for the Sergeant in charge of the West Black Isle area.

There is some correspondence available between Sgt Henderson and his senior officers regarding his duties. The letters are handwritten and although they state the date and month the letters are written, they don't state the year. The following two letters might have been written in the run-up to, or during, the First World War.

While James was serving at Muir of Ord, his senior officer wrote him a letter informing him that there might be someone intent on espionage in the Muir of Ord area. *"I am informed that there is a person employed as a labourer at the farm of Balloan of whom persons in the district are suspicious that he is not what he appears to be. It is said that he gets, and sends away, a large number of letters."* The letter goes on to give the man's name and Sgt Henderson is asked to make urgent enquiries about his behaviour.

A second letter was sent to Sgt Henderson regarding a Viscountess residing in the Conon Hotel, Conon Bridge. Sgt

Henderson is asked to interview the lady as she has been seen taking photographs of HM Ships at Cromarty. He is instructed to point out to her that she is committing an offence under the Defence of the Realm Act and that the Naval Intelligence Department at Cromarty have the matter in hand. The letter ends: *"This lady's chauffeur may be able to give some explanation."*

A letter headed *"Bones found at Kessock"* was also received by Sgt Henderson from his senior officer. *"I observe from the local newspaper today an account of mysterious findings of bones in the course of some excavations at Kessock Ferry."* The letter goes on to ask if Sgt Henderson has made any enquiries into this and if so *"…I am surprised you have sent me no report of the*

circumstances." The bones had apparently been found in quicklime. A search of the local newspapers for reports of the foregoing incidents has found nothing.

On 5th June 1914 James was promoted to Detective Sergeant and transferred to Headquarters in Dingwall. This was apparently a war-related supernumerary position and at the end of the war James returned to his previous position as Sergeant in Muir of Ord.

In 1922 Sgt Henderson was transferred to Fortrose where he remained until his retirement on 25th October 1939, after thirty-seven years' police service.

James married Mary Grant in Tain on 8th June 1906 and went on to have five daughters. His grandchildren George and Marlene Skinner were brought up in Rosemarkie but moved away. They still holiday in Rosemarkie and Fortrose from time to time. Grandchildren David Brooks and Dorothy MacDonald (nee Brooks) live in Fortrose.

James died at Rosemarkie in 1955 and is buried in Rosemarkie Churchyard.

James Henderson and Mary Grant who were married in June 1906.

Snippets Some jottings from the author's notebook

The Sloug

My father called it "The Sloug". Some Rosemarkie people call it "The Slog", so who's right? And could it have been called "The Slug"? I often wondered where the path and steps leading from Courthill Road to the bottom of the Manse Brae got their name, but no-one could give me a satisfactory answer.

Whilst doing some research in the Highland Council Archives recently, I might have found the answer. I was reading the minutes of the Fortrose Town Council. In a report dated 10th October 1898, the Council was renewing the annual rents for various pieces of land in and around Fortrose and Rosemarkie. The annual rent for "*the pasture of Common Slug at Rosemarkie…*" was being renewed by Mr R J Gillanders, but the report gave no indication of where the piece of ground could be. Mr Gillanders lived in Crawmarkie, Courthill Road. I wondered if this piece of ground was the strip of land to the south of The Sloug at Courthill Road and which in 1898 could have been common land.

When I checked the Concise Scots Dictionary I found that a Slock or Slug is a pass or a hollow between hills, and a Slogg is a marsh or bog. The Slug is also the name of the road through the pass between Banchory and Stonehaven. I checked out the old maps of the area but could find no trace of any land called The Slug or The Slog in Rosemarkie.

Fort George and the Rosemarkie Gun

On 13th July 1891 the Town Council minutes recorded that "*a report has been published of a proposal to dismantle Fort George.*" The council was opposed to this and agreed to organise a petition against the proposal.

The plans to dismantle must have got under way because in November 1891 the Town Council corresponded with War Office officials with a view to obtaining one of the large guns at Fort George for ornamental purposes. The War Office offered the Town Council an eighteen-pound single-barrelled gun and iron carriage for £5, the cost of transport to be paid by the Town Council. Mr John Hossack of Gollanhead offered to pay for the gun, providing it was placed in Rosemarkie, and Baillie George Sutherland, Rosemarkie, agreed to arrange and pay for the transportation.

The gun stood for many years at the back of Rosemarkie Parish Church, facing out towards Fort George, until it was requisitioned during the Second World War and melted down for the war effort.

Mr Fletcher's Trees

In the Council minutes of 4th September 1889, it was reported that Mr Fletcher of Rosehaugh offered to present the Burgh with young trees to plant along both sides of the road between Fortrose and Rosemarkie, provided the Town Council accepted them and arranged to protect them.

The Council unanimously thanked Mr Fletcher for his kind offer and agreed to get consent of the various proprietors owning the land on both sides of the road. Nothing more was heard of this proposal until 14th April 1890 when an entry states: "*Provost Grant moved that the town council will take up the offer of the trees…*" But by now they were to be planted "*…along the roadsides in Fortrose within the Burgh, and on both sides of the bleaching green at Castle grounds and Bishop Shod.*" There is no mention of the Rosemarkie road.

The Rosemarkie Fever Cases

I found an interesting snippet in the council minutes of a

special meeting on 1st November 1897 which, I think, involved my great-granny and her family. Rosemarkie was in the grip of a fever epidemic and, with there being no hospital available nearby to treat the cases, it was proposed to: "...have Mrs More and family removed from the room at Mr MacRae's coach-house to be thoroughly cleaned and made comfortable for receipt of patients and prevent disease." I suppose this was the nearest thing Rosemarkie had to a hospital. My great-granny moved in with her parents at 5 Bridge Street and lived there until she died in 1953

The Schooner *Louisa*

In 1852 the schooner *Louisa* was launched at Rosemarkie. According to the Register of Ships at Inverness Port she was built, at Rosemarkie, by John Cook, Shipbuilder, Inverness. At sixty-nine tons, square-sterned with one deck and two masts, rigged with a standing bowsprit, *Louisa* was a sailing vessel. The framework and planking were of wood and she had a female figurehead. The skipper was John Henderson.

According to Alistair Fraser in his booklet *Random Notes of Old Rosemarkie*, the *Louisa* was built of larch from the woods at Raddery and was named after Mrs Louisa Fowler of Raddery.

The information recorded in the Register of Shipping named the owner of the *Louisa* as Kenneth MacKenzie, Junior, merchant in Rosemarkie who held sixty-four shares. John Ross of Cromarty became a part-owner on 11th May 1852 when Kenneth MacKenzie transferred thirty-two shares to him and in September 1852 a further thirty-two shares were transferred to John Ross. Hugh MacIntosh became Master in 1856. The final entry in the register reports that *Louisa* was lost off Whitby in 1868.

I found the following article in the *Aberdeen Journal* dated Saturday 28th January 1868: "*On Wednesday morning the Schooner Briton (Captain Mockett) of and from Portsmouth, arrived at Hartlepool with a boat and crew of four men of the Schooner Louisa of Inverness, abandoned off Robin Hood's Bay on Tuesday morning. Their vessel having sprung a leak, they were forced to take to their boat where they had been seven hours during a strong gale...*"

The Colonel's Woody

On 23rd December 1858, an application was received from Colonel Hector MacKenzie for permission to plant trees on the land stretching from his property in Academy Street, down to the sea.

The Town Council claimed ownership of the land bordering the sea, and they had provided fifty stone steps, at a cost of £10, for public access. However, after considering the application, the Magistrates decided that Colonel MacKenzie's plans for planting would be a great improvement to the area and, provided the path and steps remained open to the public, they unanimously approved the project.

The Colonel's Woody still exists, but is incorporated into the gardens of the various houses which have since been built on the land.

Photo Album

Wedding of Barbara Elder and William Skinner. From left: Maureen Young, Elizabeth Anderson, William and Barbara, Jimmy Skinner, Doreen Elder, Shona Elder.

Wedding photo of Jenny Jack and Dan Paterson, 1951. Best man John Paterson, brother of groom; groom Dan Paterson, bride Jenny Jack; Bridesmaid Betty Jack (cousin of bride); Isobel Paterson (niece of groom). At front: Clare White, nephew of groom; William and Kenneth Jack, nephews of bride.

British Legion Bus Trip To Strathpeffer 1960. Front row, from left: Mr and Mrs Willie Fraser; Donnie and Katy-Mary Sutherland; Margaret and Hugh MacKenzie; Mrs MacKeddie; Rhoda MacNeil; Mr Hay, Fortrose. Second row from front: ?; ?; Isa MacKeddie; ?; Min Ross (Mrs Leitham); James McNeil. Third row from front: Margaret MacKenzie (Munro); Mrs MacKay (wife of Bunty); Caroline Anderson; Mrs Evelyn Sutherland; Mrs Ross (mother of Rhoda MacNeil); Jack Stuart. Back row: ?; Willie MacLeman; Fred Lenz (in hat); ?; Donnie Sutherland; ?; Mr Ross (Rhoda MacNeil's father).

Wedding of Edith More and Mark Grigor 1958. Piper is Jessie Cumming.

Fortrose Academy 1959/60. Back row, from left: Geordie Swanson; Keith Young; Sandy Alexander. Middle: George Skinner; Ralph Leitch; Valerie Campbell; Ann MacDonald; Sandy Patience; James Anderson; Alistair Bassindale. Front row: Dougie MacKay; Rory Smart; Rhoda Fraser; Sarella Gallie; Margaret Munro (Ardmeanach); Sylvia Brookes (MacKay); Graham Jack.

Jenny Paterson, Betty Smith and Rhoda Anderson selling white heather in aid of the Scottish Children's League of Pity.

Jenny Paterson and Rhoda Anderson all dolled up to go to a wedding.

The postman and Miller family at Blackstand Croft, c1900. Back row. from left: Postman, Esther, Roddy and John Miller. John Miller is the father of Jean MacArthur, Rosemarkie. Front: Bella (or it may be Teen), Christina (nee Bisset) and Ann.

Councillor Charles James Spurgeon MacKenzie. On 9th July 1970, Charles MacKenzie was made a Burgess and Freeman of the Royal Burgh of Fortrose in thanks for his loyal and faithful service to the Burgh as Councillor and Magistrate, 1927-1970.

Mabel Fraser (nee Anderson). Mabel ran the Post Office in Rosemarkie for many years.

Minnie and Ernest Leitham. Ernest and Min met when they were in the same class in school in Fortrose. Ernest joined the merchant navy and was a stoker on both the *Queen Mary* and *Queen Elizabeth*.

Party in the Royal Hotel, Fortrose to celebrate Roy MacCormack leaving for a new life in America. Back row, from left: Alec Young; Dodo Wilson; Bob MacLean; Billy MacIntosh; Hugh (Toorie) More; Billy MacKay; Davie Watt; David Ainslie; Rossie MacDonald; Bob MacKeddie; Archie Lumsden; Davie Munro; Jimmy Ritchie. Middle: Dorothy MacDonald (Brookes); Betty Watt; Katy-Mary Sutherland; Betty Young; Roy MacCormack; Mary MacIntosh; wife of Bob MacKeddie; Margaret Ritchie. Front: Teen More; May MacLean; Rhoda Wilson (Anderson); Lilian MacKay; Jimmy MacIntosh; wife of Archie Lumsden; wife of David Ainslie.

Fortrose Town Council. The photo is thought to have been taken sometime in the 1960s at the Marine Hotel Rosemarkie, but no-one can remember what the occasion was. Back row, from left: George Lackie; Dod Young; Attie Matheson; Ian Cameron; Jock Owens; Murdo MacPhail; Archie Stirling. Front: Jean Hay; Mrs MacDonald (Buntait); Agnes Cheyne; Provost Harry Rogers; Margaret Crawford; Jimmy Currie; Margaret Hamilton; John MacKay.

Willie Young (Willie Foof), Sandy Wightman and Rod Anderson. Willie Young lived in Marine Cottage (now called Turnstone) and in his later years did odd jobs such as helping with the salmon fishing and working as a relief postman. He liked a dram or two, and one New Year's Day he was found stranded in a ditch up at Raddery, surrounded by the contents of his post bag. He was gathered up and taken home! Sandy Wightman came to live in Seaforth Cottage when he moved here from Fife on his retirement.

See separate section on Rod Anderson.

Mrs MacAndrew's shop and Post Office on Mill Road. The building no longer exists, but once stood on the piece of ground next to the Plough Inn, which is now used as a sitting-out area for the pub. You can see the side of Seafield at the rear and the edge of the Plough Inn to the left of the photo. The lady is most probably Jeannie MacAndrew.

Members of Fortrose Fire
Station personnel taken at
Avoch Gala Day, July 1959.
Back row, from left: Arthur
MacArthur, Alistair
Campbell, Robert MacRae.
Front row: Dodo Wilson,
Fowler Wilson, Donnie
Cameron.

Sandy Hossack and Janet Grigor who were married on 18th September 1969.

The Highland Bus Company Dance in Inverness in March 1958. From left: Peg and Alec (The Lairdie) MacKenzie; Rhoda and Dodo Wilson; Helen Duncan (nee MacKenzie).

Rosemarkie Ladies Football Team. Back row, from left: Sheila Paterson (nee MacKenzie); Edith Grigor (nee More); Anne MacIver (nee Anderson); Evelyn Topp (nee Fraser); Marlene Skinner. Shirley Black (nee Campbell). Front: Doreen Doull (nee Bassindale); Valerie MacLean (nee Campbell); Irene Patience (nee Ewen); Sylvia Brooks (nee MacKay); Sandra Jack (nee Garrow).

Threshing at the Ness about 1939. Isobel Grigor is the little girl at the front and the woman on the extreme right is her aunt, Jessie Young.

Alice Sutherland,
Isobel Grigor and
John Reddigan.

John Reddigan in his heyday.

Johnnie and the Diamonds sometime in the 1960s. David Brooks, Hugh MacKenzie, Jack Sutherland and, at the back, John Reddigan.

Davy MacKay, barman in the Plough Inn, Rosemarkie, 1974.

I've been unable to identify the two boys standing at the door of the Plough Inn. The public bar was renovated recently and, as one of the engraved glass panels on the inside door was cracked, both panels were removed and replaced with plain glass. The panels are protected, however, and the owners of the pub are not allowed to destroy them. They are stored in a room in the Plough with a view to finding a way to display them in the pub in the future.

Lorna Kemp was crowned Valentine Mum at a dance in the Gordon Memorial Hall sometime in the 1960s. She is pictured with her husband, Frankie, and judges Jane and Jimmy Holm of Rosemarkie.